Guiding the Gifted Child

Studies in

EDUCATION

RANDOM HOUSE

New York

Guiding the Gifted Child

by George I. Thomas
New York State Education Department

and Joseph Crescimbeni
Jacksonville University

To our wives,

MAVIS *and* ALYNE

Preface

This book is an exposition on the needs, expectations and problems encountered with gifted children in the classroom. It represents an attempt to identify, characterize and understand the nature of gifted children. It discusses procedures used by educators for the recognition of gifted children other than the often-used intelligence test. Furthermore, it presents a *plan of action* for meeting the needs of gifted pupils through acceleration and enrichment.

The improvement of instruction, evaluation techniques and teaching materials has brought into focus more clearly the existence of gifted children. The need for the improvement of teaching techniques for gifted children has necessitated a more thorough understanding and analysis of their role in the school curriculum.

It is the hope of the authors that this book will foster a new impetus to the teacher who discovers gifted children under her supervision. The suggestions and recommendations presented are classroom-tested measures that should prove successful in most American schools.

GEORGE I. THOMAS
and JOSEPH CRESCIMBENI

January, 1966

Contents

part one | *Discovering the Characteristics and Educational Needs of Gifted Children*

1 The Challenge of Giftedness

Educators have known for many years that gifted children have inner resources which make them potentially superior to most of their peermates. Unfortunately for purposes of identification, these children come in many sizes and shapes, which can be most disconcerting to those who are looking for stereotypes. Though they may have widely different traits, the most commonly accepted characteristic of gifted boys and girls is intellectual superiority.

The term *gifted* may apply to pupils with IQ's that start with 115 and range as high as 200. The Educational Policies Commission suggests that pupils with IQ's of 137 or above be considered highly gifted and that moderately gifted pupils be classified as having IQ's ranging from 120 to 137. In many educational circles the term *moderately gifted* has been specifically applied to pupils having IQ's ranging from 115 to 135. If this lower range is accepted, educators must be prepared to provide for the special needs of 15 to 20 per cent of the total school population when they talk about programs for gifted children. If they take the former figure, 120 to 137, they must be prepared to do something extra for about 10 per cent of the pupil population. In addition, they must be prepared to do something special for the 1 to 2 per cent of the school population falling into the highly gifted category. A number of special classes for gifted children require a minimum IQ of 135 for consideration and admittance. Terman used 140 as a standard for inclusion in his special experimental class while Hollingworth accepted 130 as one index.

There is also a tendency to accept intellectual capacity as an indication of giftedness without considering the different abilities of children with different capacities. Thus, one pupil with an IQ of 150 may have a high verbal ability and a low mathematical ability while another may have a high mathematical ability and a low verbal ability. A third pupil with an IQ of 150 may have artistic ability in the field of music, but in no other area. There are so many variables to consider when one thinks of children in terms of IQ's that some educators are loathe to use classifications based upon mere intelligence. Some of them are concerned about the cultural impact upon pupil test scores and refer to studies that indicate that the true IQ may not be obtained when children from impoverished homes or low economic areas are tested. Other educators are reluctant to use the results of a single intelligence test to classify children since different tests measure different types of ability. Again, different tests have different limits, so some children will appear to have a greater capacity than other children, depending upon the nature of the test used.

Nationwide, the gifted and talented pupils may take in 20 to 30 per cent of our school population. From this group one can expect to obtain a large number of the scientists, artists, musicians, writers, actors, craftsmen, lawyers, doctors, political leaders, educators and business leaders. This segment of our school population includes most of our best thinkers or at least those individuals who have the potential to work in abstract realms. These children are the ones who should be making the *A's* in the average classroom. Because of their superior intellect they are capable of abstract reasoning with little, if any, teacher help, as long as they are guided properly from one learning level to another. They have the capacity to perform numerous processes mentally that are considered laborious for average pupils. This ability is a tremendous time-saver in the learning situation. These boys and girls are able to think in terms of symbols or groups of situations instead of specific data or concrete objects. They can leave behind many concrete and physical aids considered essential to success for pupils of lower ability; however, some of these children may enjoy continued experiences with concrete objects because of the element of change in the teaching process. The novelty appeal may be more important to bright pupils than the actual concepts taught through the manipulative process.

But the intellectual ability of students as measured by their IQ is not always a valid criterion. Often it is not so easy to identify such individuals because they may possess many of the same attributes, interests or characteristics as average and slow-learning students. When achievement is measured in terms of an expectancy level for a given level of intelligence, students who need help in reading, speech, writing, or arithmetic may be classified as underachievers or slow learners. This is due to the failure of the individual pupil to reveal his true potential or level of achievement and understanding in a formal testing situation. A poor language background or the inability to read may be considered as a deterrent to the identification of creativity or intellectual giftedness. Again, a lack of motivation or exposure to faulty instructional approaches by lower grade teachers may become barriers to the identification of the true capacity of gifted children. Frequently, boys and girls who fall into a retarded or remedial classification are referred to a school psychologist for help when they reach the intermediate or upper grades. This may be their first exposure to a testing instrument that probes beyond the language barrier with the result that high mental capacity will be revealed that

Figure   PROJECTED DISTRIBUTION OF INTELLIGENCE IN THE UNITED STATES BASED
ON A POPULATION OF 200,000,000

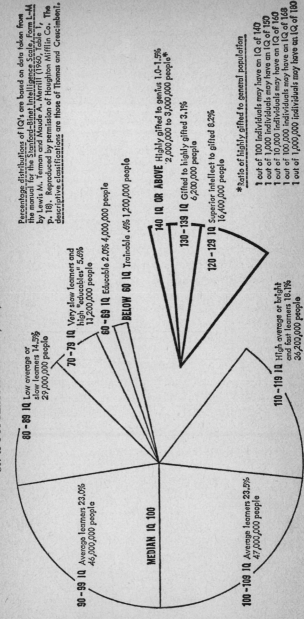

Percentage distributions of IQ's are based on data taken from the manual for the Stanford-Binet Intelligence Scale, Form L-M by Lewis M. Terman and Maude A. Merrill (1960), Table 1, p. 18). Reproduced by permission of Houghton Mifflin Co. The descriptive classifications are those of Thomas and Crescimbeni.

140 IQ OR ABOVE Highly gifted to genius 1.0-1.5%*
2,000,000 to 3,000,000 people

130 - 139 IQ Gifted to highly gifted 3.1%
6,200,000 people

120 - 129 IQ Superior intellect to gifted 8.2%
16,400,000 people

110 - 119 IQ High average or bright and fast learners 18.1%
36,200,000 people

100 - 109 IQ Average learners 23.5%
47,000,000 people

MEDIAN IQ 100

90 - 99 IQ Average learners 23.0%
46,000,000 people

80 - 89 IQ Low average or slow learners 14.5%
29,000,000 people

70 - 79 IQ Very slow learners and high "educables" 5.6%
11,200,000 people

60 - 69 IQ Educable 2.0% 4,000,000 people

BELOW 60 IQ Trainable .6% 1,200,000 people

*Ratio of highly gifted to general population

1 out of 100 individuals may have an IQ of 140
1 out of 1,000 individuals may have an IQ of 150
1 out of 10,000 individuals may have an IQ of 160
1 out of 100,000 individuals may have an IQ of 168
1 out of 1,000,000 individuals may have an IQ of 180

was overlooked by classroom teachers who depend on group intelligence or group achievement tests. By this time faulty work patterns and poor attitudes may have been so firmly established that it is too late to overcome the academic deficiencies that will enable the pupils to achieve at levels commensurate with their true potential.

Another problem for educators lies in distinguishing between gifted and highly extroverted pupils who memorize easily or are extremely vocal. In many instances teachers refer to these students as the "fast learners," "the boys and girls in the top group" or the "brighter children." A large number of these pupils *may* be classified as intellectually gifted; however, there is a danger that the teachers will overlook the shy, withdrawn student who grasps concepts rapidly but cannot demonstrate his skill to perceive or comprehend. Involved here are motivational and emotional factors that operate very strongly in determining the response of individual students to a learning situation.

Another problem in characterizing giftedness comes in classifying children who are not intellectually gifted in their overall ability but who are talented or potentially gifted in one particular subject or aspect of learning. These students may be creative or imaginative or talented in a way that makes them outstanding in esthetic undertakings, but slow and unresponsive to the more academic subjects. Often these are the students who do exceptionally well in one aspect of an IQ test and below average in the other sections.

Then, there are the moderately gifted boys and girls with IQ's ranging from 120 to 135 who are usually welcome members of the class, but teachers are not inclined to think of them as gifted children. They tend to be the fast workers, the ones who can accept a direction once it is given without needless repetition. It can be such a pleasure to work with them that the teacher wishes all her children could work as successfully and as easily as they do. In such classes the gifted pupil who is a nonconformist will tend to rate low in the esteem of the teacher. His potential is apt to be lost because his marks are often lower than those received by his conformist peermates. He is often penalized by teachers who become insecure by his mere presence in a class.

The Nature of the Gifted Child

Thus, there are problems not only in classifying gifted children, but subsequently in meeting their needs. Since only 1 to 2 per cent of the total school population may belong to the highly gifted classification (those easily recognizable, with IQ's above 140), many teachers never come in contact with such individuals in their classrooms. This is especially true when we realize that most gifted children are just boys and girls trying to live a normal life. They tend to find many satisfactions in both academic and non-academic activities. The fact that they have high intelligence quotients does not make them into curiosities or freaks. While studies have shown that those most highly endowed intellectually may have more difficult adjustments to make than those falling into the superior category, both types of students can fit into group activities without creating problems for teachers or peermates of lesser ability. For the most part gifted children tend to be equal and, in many instances, superior to average boys and girls in health, physical development, emotional stability and social maturity. The small, puny, "bulgy-eyed" characters tend to be exceptions to the rule. Records show that they are likely to be physically stronger and have a stronger resistance to illness than average boys and girls. They can be friendly and outgoing, or they may be shy and withdrawn. Some may be extremely studious, but others appear to have little interest in their studies. The following table summarizes some of the common myths associated with giftedness and their concomitant rebuttals based on fact.

Table 1   THE NATURE OF THE GIFTED CHILD—
FACT AND FANCY

The stereotype of the gifted child—fancy	*The gifted child teachers actually see and work with in the classroom—fact*
1. The gifted child is just an oddball or freak.	Most gifted children are so normal that teachers often fail to identify them as being gifted pupils.
2. Gifted children are weak and puny. They are not very athletic, because they are not strong and healthy.	They tend to be stronger, have less illness, are as tall, if not taller, as heavy, if not heavier than their less gifted peermates; and they take part in a wide variety of activities that call for vigor. Many are outstanding athletes.
3. The gifted child is always a bookworm. He always has a book under his arm, wears glasses and lacks time for normal children's activities.	Most gifted children are good readers and find many answers in the world of books; but they engage in many types of activities, have many interests and hobbies. Others do not read and may actually need remedial help in order to read up to grade level.
4. The gifted child is the one who is most enthusiastic about school and school work.	Many gifted pupils are enthusiastic about school, but others are not, as is evidenced by their failure to go on to college or even to complete high school.
5. Gifted children never develop into good-looking young women or handsome young men. The "brain" is seldom pictured as being attractive. He wears thick, horn-rimmed glasses and does not know what good grooming means.	Some of the best-looking men and women in America are to be found among gifted adults. Brains and good looks often go together. No one group of boys and girls possesses a monopoly on good looks. Many athletes, actors, and actresses who are the ideal for boys and girls as well as adults have very high IQ's along with their physical attractions and characteristics.

The stereotype of the gifted child—fancy	*The gifted child teachers actually see and work with in the classroom—fact*
6. Nearly all gifted children come from upper, middle class, and professional families. Teachers won't find them coming from the lower social and economic levels.	Gifted children come from all walks of life with three fourths of those rated above average actually coming from families whose parents have occupations below that of the professional or highly successful businessman. Since there are more average and below-average families, many prodigies are lost in the crowd.
7. Gifted children will usually be the best-dressed and best-mannered youngsters in the class.	Many gifted children come from poor families and may be overlooked because they dress poorly or have a different set of living standards.
8. Gifted children "ripen early and rot early." They never amount to much when they become adults. Most of them will be failures in their adult life.	The Terman studies and the Stanford studies show outstanding success achieved by gifted individuals. An unusual proportion of them became lawyers, doctors, engineers, college professors and leaders in government, business and industry.
9. Gifted children are "queer." They are usually crazy, they do not know what they are doing. "They're wacky."	Studies show that gifted people are apt to be highly stable individuals. Only a small proportion of them ever spend time in a mental institution. A few may be eccentric, but so are many of the nongifted.
10. Gifted children are social misfits. They do not know how to behave in a social situation.	Gifted boys and girls tend to enjoy social situations. They talk readily and know a great deal about many topics or fields of study. They are good mixers and tend to assume more than their share of social leadership roles in school and out of it.
11. The play interests and activities of gifted children	Studies show that gifted children have the same interests

The stereotype of the gifted child—fancy	*The gifted child teachers actually see and work with in the classroom—fact*
are unlike those of normal children.	and indulge in the same kind of play that normal children do. They enjoy out-of-door games more than they do indoor games; however, they may prefer more complicated and more competitive games than do children of lower ability.
12. Gifted children are apt to be egotistic and snobbish.	Most gifted children have desirable personalities. They tend to be more courteous, get along better with their peermates, are more obedient and will take suggestions faster than other children will.
13. Gifted children who have the same IQ's tend to have the same kind of abilities and academic interests.	Individual differences among gifted children make it difficult to put them in homogeneous classes with the expectation that they will all achieve at the same levels. Pupils with the same abilities can be far apart when it comes to interests, capacities and needs. Each pupil's pattern of abilities and talents is quite unique.
14. Gifted children are not very successful when they have to do handicraft work.	Gifted pupils who are given opportunities to engage in activities calling for handicraft skill at the same time that average and below-average pupils do will find greater satisfaction in such activities and will achieve higher standards of work than normal children.
15. Gifted boys and girls never become leaders in the elementary or secondary school.	The ability to lead is a characteristic of many gifted children. Many boys and girls who are leaders have a higher intelligence quotient than those

The stereotype of the gifted child—fancy	*The gifted child teachers actually see and work with in the classroom—fact*
	they lead. Gifted children tend to be more interested in people than average pupils are.
16. Gifted boys and girls often fail to adjust to college, if they are accelerated through elementary or secondary schools, because of their immaturity.	While some gifted young men and women may have problems in college if they are accelerated, the studies of such pupils show that they can make very good adjustments if they are not accelerated more than two years above their peers in chronological age.
17. Gifted children are often timid, shy and anxious individuals. They are generally afraid of their own shadows.	Nongifted children are often bothered by more anxieties than gifted children because they cannot always anticipate trouble in time to avert it. The gifted pupil is able to see trouble coming in time to change his behavioral pattern and thereby avert trouble. As a result, he has less anxiety and fear than less capable peermates.

Teachers who find enjoyment and challenge in their work will often see the difference in their own attitudes towards a class if they have bright students to keep things moving. Such pupils liven up discussions and continue to make worthwhile contributions. Unfortunately, these same teachers may overlook the quiet, retiring pupils who may want to emulate their more outgoing classmates but who still feel insecure and uncertain about the best way to show that they have special abilities or talents. Every pupil in the heterogeneous class can benefit from the stimulation supplied by a few extremely bright pupils. Much has been said about the waste of intellect when gifted students are left in heterogeneous classrooms. But it cannot be overlooked that these pupils have a great deal to gain from working in an atmosphere where they can excel and be acknowledged as leaders. This opportunity for leadership can be lost when they are placed in classes where everyone is a general and there are no privates, lieutenants, captains or majors.

On the other hand, there are some extremely gifted individuals who do not want to stand out. For example, the truly talented pupil may find that his greatest satisfactions come when he is given freedom to work alone. He requires large blocks of uninterrupted time to read, to listen, to think and to create (write, paint, draw, experiment). This does not mean that he is socially or emotionally immature. It may be that he is just a very highly creative person who needs solitude to realize his goals. He may have the ability to concentrate for long periods of time and submerge himself completely in challenging activities, or he may simply be reluctant to thrust himself into highly organized, competitive learning situations. In this case, he may require some extra help in becoming a member of a small work group or team.

In the case of talented children who are not intellectually gifted, the school staff will have to use a different approach. The truly creative student may have to learn to apply his special skills to the interpretation and understanding of the world as revealed in the academically structured classroom. In contrast, many intellectually gifted students must be given the experiences that lead to creative action. And they will have to learn that there is a time when personal values may have to take priority over those of the teacher.

Teachers have been urged to push gifted children. We do need our scientists and our artists, but talented individuals can be destroyed when they are pressured in the same manner as the intellectually gifted. Similarly, the truly gifted may resist the pressure to follow a strong math or science-oriented program when he has other interests. In many communities there is constant pressure to promote creativity when in actuality the facilities are inadequate or the teaching staff is unprepared to give youngsters opportunities to explore, experiment or merely to enjoy new fields of interest.

Gifted children are curious about the world around them. This is often evident in the questions they ask, the variety of materials they use to obtain information and the breadth of their interests. Many of them may be noted for their hobbies. In many homes it is not a matter of one single hobby but several. They collect coins, stamps, rocks, signatures, books, magazines, guns and other articles of interest. In addition to collecting material things they collect information until they become experts about a wide range of subjects. In one school, a girl became an authority about horses, their histories, illnesses, characteristics, care and use to man. In another, a boy made model airplanes and could tell a listener about the history of early aviation, the names and exploits of noted fliers, the types of planes used for private or military purposes and their general strengths or weaknesses. Their interests often lead them to ask *how* or *why* and *when*. When necessary, they show extremely high powers of concentration and exert a tremendous amount of energy to obtain answers that satisfy them.

Teachers can frequently capitalize on their wide interests to get them started in higher-level research activities. For the most part, the gifted students welcome a challenge, especially when they see reasons for their actions and the possibility of attaining desired goals. They enjoy a full life and frequently try to pack so many experiences into a day that adults may have to direct them to develop an experience in depth rather than scatter their energies. At other times, they need to be motivated by an understanding adult before they venture into new fields of study or activity. They can and will take directions from adults they respect, adults who are sincere and fair in their relations with them.

Intellectually gifted children frequently possess multiple-track rather than single-track minds. This means that some of them are apt to be most adept in recalling names, facts, ideas and processes through the use of association instead of by simple, unaided recall. Ability along this line can give them a tremendous advantage over less talented peermates who have a very high forgetting curve. As a result, they can study topics more intensively and retain more information for a longer period of time without having to devote monotonous hours to reviewing or drilling in order to give a report or take a test. They still review, but how they study and for how long will depend upon their goals and interests. While the average learner may be satisfied if he can pass, the gifted pupil often has the desire to maintain a rank at the top performance levels. His goal is, thus, excellence or outstanding performance instead of survival.

Intellectually gifted students tend to prefer an opportunity to work with long units of work rather than short ones. They can work for extended periods of time and with little diminishing of enthusiasm whereas less capable pupils are apt to lose interest if the teacher does not break their work patterns by introducing them to new and shorter units of work. As a rule, gifted students prefer long-term assignments to day-by-day study and recitation activities. They can make decisions on their own and do not need to have the teacher constantly looking over their shoulders. They need and welcome teacher help and encouragement, but they can frequently detect their own mistakes or find motivation for extended activity in a particular field of study.

Research studies show that intellectually gifted boys and girls often can read rapidly and with a high rate of comprehension when they are in the elementary grades, but these same individuals may have limited reading tastes or backgrounds when they reach high school. Again, they may be able to dominate in a class discussion because they have mastered required assignments, but their actual thinking may be a mere translation of what they have heard or read instead of being something which comes from within. In both instances, their lack of depth may reflect the type of school experiences that they have encountered as members of classes where pupils were not motivated to extend their interests or to experiment with ideas.

Gifted pupils may develop rapidly in many directions, but their growth can still be uneven. Thus, a student may read widely in areas where he has special interests but will make little effort to read about topics the teacher feels are important unless she can find some motivating force to give him a balanced background. With help and guidance coming at the right time and in the right place, these boys and girls can develop the necessary means for making a successful life adjustment. Because they are *individuals*, the classroom teacher will often find that she has to vary her approach with them. Talking *with* them as well as *to* them will suffice to get boys and girls working on a particular project, but there will be times when she cannot get through to them. If she orders them to do something without telling them why, they may do what she says, but without the enthusiasm they show when they understand why they are being asked to spend their time and energy on a given assignment. This resistance is most often evident when boys and girls are asked to perform routine mechanical activities that do not require much in the way of intellectual ability.

Employers have noted a tendency on the part of intelligent workers to perform less efficiently on routine assembly line jobs than workers with only average or even below-average intelligence. The classroom teacher will frequently find that gifted pupils do not perform at high levels in areas based upon routine and meaningless drill. This resistance may become evident in the lack of interest in perfecting handwriting skills based upon traditional exercises. Gifted children may show high mechanical skills that can lead to a future position in the field of art, engineering or science, but they differ from average students in that they may bring a creative element to their work. They may readily discover short cuts when a job becomes distasteful. They will note, for example, small details that excite their imagination. They can see likenesses and differences without having to be told and then may want to modify a standard procedure. This ability to think and reason is what gets in their way on routine jobs. With help they can develop good penmanship and typing skills, but the extremely gifted are likely to be somewhat impatient when mechanical dexterity comes slowly. The good reader will frequently see the desirability of going back to the world of books.

One of the stereotypes of the past shows gifted boys and girls as misfits or bunglers when it comes to athletics, but this is far from the fact. These children tend to be stronger, have less illness, are as tall if not taller, as heavy if not heavier than their less intellectually favored peermates. When these characteristics are supplemented by a good brain and high motivation plus training, the athletic world cannot ignore them. In many instances, however, potential athletes of the calibre of Willie Mays or Sonja Henie fail to obtain the recognition that is due them because of the failure of academically-minded teachers to recognize athletic talent or to provide adequate training at an early age. Good physical education programs should start with the first grade, not to identify and develop young athletes but to insure balanced physical growth as well as intellectual growth. If such programs are delayed until the onset of puberty, the lack of early muscular development and the acquisition of skills necessary for acceptance in team activity will create problems for potentially talented boys and girls. Insecurity, awkwardness, fear of ridicule and conflicting value standards become barriers to success on the athletic field. Generally speaking, the high school or college athlete who does show that he can earn high grades in the classroom or score high on achievement tests finds that less capable peermates will not hold his studiousness against him whereas they may be somewhat less receptive to the brilliant student who shuns athletics than those who forego so-called higher interests for competition on the playground and athletic fields.

Another common stereotype centers around the term

looks. The gifted girl is not supposed to be very good-looking, nor is the boy supposed to be well-built and handsome. Here again the public fails to recognize their physical advantages and natural attractions because some gifted students fail to pay attention to their good features. This is where an individual's varied interests and intense drive in several directions provide satisfactions that make attention to dress seem unimportant. There is a tendency among bright college girls to defer marriage until they are twenty-one or twenty-two years old while the average non-college girl is married at eighteen or nineteen. Here values are involved: marriage is less important to the collegiate than the non-collegiate girl; therefore, she does not place as much emphasis on displaying her figure for the edification of boys. The observer on the Wellesley campus on Wednesdays and Thursdays will seldom recognize the informally attired students as the beautiful butterflies floating around the ballroom floor on Friday or Saturday night in the arms of gallant, good-looking young men from Harvard, Princeton, M.I.T. and other more remote college campuses. Our college-bound pupils have what it takes in the way of good looks—they just defer advertising it.

Gifted children are often characterized as hard to get along with, but studies have shown that this is far from the truth. They have normal interests and are not regarded by their associates as being peculiar or odd. They tend to take part in more social activities than their less capable peermates and assume more than their share of leadership roles both in and out of school. Terman and others (in Volume I of their *Genetic Studies of Genius*) have shown that gifted children tend to be more popular and more socially active than boys and girls coming from other intellectual groups; however, Hollingworth seems to feel that boys and girls in the 130 to 150 IQ range will find greater acceptance and understanding on the part of less capable peermates than the extremely gifted who deviate markedly in their intellect with others. Thus, the boy with the 175 IQ may find it difficult to make contact or find anyone who really understands him while the boy with the 135 IQ adjusts to the interests of the group with which he is in close and daily communication.

It has been found that gifted children at the elementary school level tend to find greater social acceptance among their peermates than do gifted children at secondary school levels. Though he may remain popular, the older student faces a greater challenge if he tries to maintain his individuality in the face of strong adolescent peer values that do not correspond to his own. At this stage some talented students, particularly girls, deliberately play down their strengths and interests to maintain status with others.

Finally, studies often show that gifted children frequently place greater value on activities which will give them satisfactions in the future than on those which give them an immediate satisfaction. The world of ideas and esthetic beauty may be much more important to them than the practical world of today with its immediate materialistic reward.

Motivating Gifted Children

What forces operate to motivate a gifted child to learn? What can be done to build within the child an intrinsic or extrinsic motivating desire to develop his talents?

Many authorities in this field believe that the intrinsic *need-to-know* or *curiosity* is a basic human motivating drive. This need-to-know, however, is not as potent as the need for *love* or *esteem*. If the needs for love and esteem are fulfilled, the gifted child is motivated by an intrinsic need to know and understand. On the other hand if the child learns that by knowing he can gain the esteem or love of others, he is motivated not for the sake of knowing or intrinsic satisfaction but because his knowing fulfills indirectly his more urgent needs.

Another major intrinsic motivating factor among the gifted is *self-actualization*. Two gifted students with iden-

tical levels of intellectual ability but with different estimates of themselves will specialize in different subjects,
have different goals and achieve different standards. Self-
concept is vital in everything the child does. The choice of
behavior, and therefore motivation, arises from the way
the student sees the world and himself. One of the most
important ways of motivating the gifted students in self-
actualization is to discuss with them their abilities, interests and vocational plans. There are many reliable tests in
these areas to help determine their particular strengths
and weaknesses. This information can serve as a basis for
motivating gifted students to do better work. The educator must be sure, however, that giving this information
is a step toward better understanding and greater motivation. Another way to help a child toward self-actualization
is to discuss his basic interests with him. An ingenious
teacher can incorporate these interests into his classroom
program. It seems unlikely that efforts to motivate will be
successful unless individual self-actualizations are well
understood.

A third intrinsic motivating device is the gifted child's
need for *achievement* or a feeling of success and accomplishment. When it is exhibited, it takes the form of
wanting to do one's best at anything or almost anything
one tries. When intense, it causes a generally high aspiration level. This need for achievement can also arise from
experiences in the family, positive ones putting an emphasis on excellence and self-fulfillment as well as negative ones that emphasize getting ahead or material success. As with the curiosity drive, the need for achievement
can arise out of the need for love or esteem, which
motivation may not always lead to intrinsic learning.

These three—curiosity, self-actualization and need for
achievement—are just some of the intrinsic influences that
motivate a gifted child to learn.

Many authorities believe that extrinsic motivating devices are equally important. The first of these extrinsic
values is *social motivation*. In every child's social environment there are a number of forces that push him

towards or away from doing his best in school. They may be his teachers, his peers or his family. The greater the social pressure, the more highly motivated the child will be to achieve. A well-liked teacher can exert a direct pressure on gifted students to do well in school, being at the same time an object of identification.

If a gifted child's peers do not value intellectual growth and academic status, the gifted child who succeeds faces the possibility of social isolation. This is a cultural problem. Therefore it takes a strong-willed child to withstand social pressure and follow his intrinsic needs to know.

The level of aspiration is closely related to social values and family experience. Terman and Oden wrote, in their study, that "no other factor so strikingly differentiates fairly successful and very successful gifted students as does the factor of family background." Family and group expectations apparently influence both the selections of goals and the success of the gifted child. He learns his values and patterns his goals more after the home than less gifted children do. A large number of families are too concerned by the uniqueness or giftedness of their child and encourage him to accept interests and goals in which his special gift is not manifested. On the other hand some families exploit the gifted child, thus interfering with his proper performance.

A second form of extrinsic motivation is *competition*. According to Freehill, there is a current tendency to recommend competition for all students and especially for the gifted child. Competition continues to place emphasis on surpassing someone; it implies attention to personal prestige, involves securing a reward proportionate to one's contribution, rather than a reward equally shared; it implies success based on the recognition of or the reward for one's achievement over others.

Advocates of competitive motivation argue its value from examples of business and material gain; children, they say, must be prepared to live in a competitive society. On the other hand, we also live in an interdependent society in which success depends as much on cooperation as it does on competition, and too much emphasis on competition can hinder the development of a child's natural tendencies.

Some gifted children may have little need to compete because their unusual abilities have been accepted in a natural way, and they desire fulfillment for personal rather than social gratification. Then there are those who may not work to their capacity for fear of the competition and comparison with others. And not all who compete truly make progress. Some students may neglect important subjects or participate in less useful activities in order to secure prizes, to be valedictorian or to achieve a certain amount of success in a particular field of work. Gifted students in a science competition may put all their effort towards making an attractive display and pay little attention to genuine scientific thought or ingenuity.

Thus, the use of vigorous competition is usually rejected because of the many negative by-products. Students afraid of losing withdraw from the very activity competition is supposed to foster while students intent on winning prizes often become devoid of social responsibility or self-criticism, and false standards frequently develop. Competition also tends to encourage aggression and hostility.

Competition can be said to have some merit where memorizing multiplication tables is concerned, but not for critical or scientific judgment. Because of the fear of failure or the attention focused on rewards, a gifted child may follow established, known procedures instead of allowing his creative and inquiring mind to explore new facets. This type of extrinsic motivation fails in precisely the areas that are most important to the gifted student.

The real issue is one of emphasis! Should the school stress prizes, marks or competition more with gifted than with average students? Experimental evidence suggests that, comparatively, gifted children profit less from competition. Therefore, it is important that students clearly understand just what is signified by a grade, an award or a pin. The value of marks is often overestimated. These are artificial extrinsic motivations, and that quality is likely to be perceived by the highly gifted child. The average child strives for a star or immediate praise, but with a gifted child the higher the level of his intellectual development, the longer he is willing to wait for his reward. We may conclude that competition cannot be used effectively for judgmental learning.

Guiding Gifted Children in the Classroom

The potentials of all kinds of gifted children should be discovered before they acquire frustrations resulting from lack of success or understanding. This will be especially true of those boys and girls who have creative talents. These children must be identified before their individuality is destroyed by school pressures and leveling influences that lead to conformity and imitation. This means that the school environment must be created that will accelerate or foster growth on the part of gifted and talented pupils in both academic and non-academic areas. Activities must, therefore, be provided that motivate a desire for learning in all young children and also meet the specific needs of those children clearly identified as gifted when they enter first grade. This will allow teachers time to work with potentially gifted children who remain hidden in a class structured on the basis of incomplete data or information. If the classroom program is a good one, many of the potentially bright pupils will leap to the challenges presented, with the result that they begin to demonstrate their ability by assuming leadership roles and by outpacing their peermates in both academic and creative achievements.

Many teachers will need special help and guidance before they can provide the depth and breadth of experiences necessary to bring out the potentialities of giftedness at kindergarten, first and second grade levels. In many elementary schools it may be necessary to modify the curriculum as well as procedures, if highly motivated children are going to continue to work close to expectation levels for their mental, social and physical ages. Some elementary school children will be placed in special gifted classes, but most small schools will lack pupils, space and the professional staff to establish them. This means that most gifted children will have to have their special needs met in normal classroom settings. The expression, "taking children where teachers find them," must become a reality instead of a cliché.

Critics will argue that talent will continue to go down the drain unless immediate steps are taken to separate and segregate intellectually gifted children from less capable peermates. But the issue is more than separation. In many instances it is a matter of *how* boys and girls are going to be taught rather than *what* they are going to be taught. So far, little attention has been paid to this phase of education, with the result that many gifted children end up in the ranks of the early school dropouts. For example, a large number of boys and girls enter kindergarten and first grade with an overwhelming desire to learn. Some of the gifted pupils will actually be reading and will, therefore, require little in the way of readiness work to prepare them for formal learning skills that they may still have to perfect. However, some of their motivation will soon be lost unless they are given ample opportunity to achieve success commensurate with their accomplishment quotients. To hold all students to the same pattern of class instruction and the same work materials is a great waste. Slow learners require many concrete experiences before they acquire a basic visual and auditory vocabulary necessary for success in reading. While some of these introductory exercises are interesting to all pupils, the intellectually mature child is capable of making a rapid transition from concrete to abstract experience; therefore, the teacher must be prepared to eliminate some stages of a beginning reading program for those individuals who demonstrate their ability to move rapidly and successfully through a basic program of study.

The very bright and superior student frequently needs guidance and direction at many learning stages more than he needs instruction. He is often able to reach achievement levels beyond those ordinarily established for a given grade with little, if any, adult assistance. However, this does not mean that he can be neglected. It may be too easy to let such students drift along because of their independence, but this is dangerous for their own well-being and development. They need to take part in a broad curriculum where the teacher shows them multiple avenues in which to grow. Basically, gifted children need to extend their worlds. The teacher's presence must be felt, but she should not constantly dominate each learning situation. As the children go from one grade to the next, they must learn the true meaning of responsible action and self-directed activity. This is something they will have to learn through actual experience over the years. It cannot be suddenly sprung on them at the sixth or seventh grade level. With training, they can learn to assume responsibility for individual, small-group and all-class activities.

Gifted children will not be neglected if they are given plenty of rich materials to work with and clear-cut directions when the teacher is not able to meet with them daily in all phases of the curriculum. Once they master basic fundamental skills, they need many opportunities to apply what they have learned in a number of different situations. These children may explore new fields of knowledge readily, but some will require the assistance of the teacher. She will have to provide the motivation to prepare them for efforts in new directions. And she must be able to build upon the strengths the students have when they come to her.

Modern educators are now advocating a type of education for *all* children that includes enrichment activities formerly limited to bright or gifted boys and girls. While this is true, it does not mean that the curriculum for gifted and nongifted children is the same.

Slow learning boys and girls require considerable repetition, but a variety of experience and interests are essential for growth and mastery. These children must read widely if they are going to acquire the practice necessary for success with the skills introduced in class. Here, enrichment may consist of activities which will lead to the mastery of basic skills and the acquisition of knowledge leading to a measure of independence.

Average boys and girls may require less repetition than their less capable peermates, but they still require many concrete experiences before they feel secure with a new skill or idea. Enrichment activities will help them expand their horizons or acquire understanding not evident in the standard text. Many of their activities will stem from new interests generated by group action. Many of these boys and girls will work very well independently, but a large number of them will require considerable teacher supervision and direction.

Gifted children need guidance, but they are capable of doing many things more independently than they are usually allowed to do in traditional classrooms. They may enjoy the same concrete experiences that slower learning peermates have, but there is a danger that they will merely go through the motions of learning. These pupils have little need for repetition and drill of the traditional type. This is where they need to engage in many broadening activities. Studies of the past show that gifted boys and girls have not always acquired high level goals. Their narrow reading interests reflect a need for stimulating and enriching experiences quite different from those provided less capable classmates. Their worlds must be extended not because they need additional practice, but to help them acquire the understanding and background leading to success with abstractions as well as with the obvious and practical.

In planning tomorrow's curriculum for gifted boys and girls, the emphasis must be on more independent action at lower grade levels. Teachers will have to encourage and direct, but they have to stop holding boys and girls back who have the ability and are ready to move to higher learning activities. Succeeding teachers must be prepared to take these fast learning students at higher learning levels. This may play havoc with graded textbooks or a traditional curriculum, but teachers must be prepared to accept the fact that gifted boys and girls are capable of traveling up the educational ladder at a fast rate of speed. With encouragement and help it is only natural for them to outdistance those working at a slower pace.

All good education must be characterized by more than a shotgun approach. All boys and girls of a given age or grade classification have many common needs and interests. These should be identified along with their specialized abilities and achievements or weaknesses in order that teaching activities can be sponsored that will foster continuous growth with a minimum waste of time and effort on the part of both student and instructor.

The work patterns and attitudes children form in the primary grades will determine to a large extent what they accomplish at upper grade levels. During the formative years constant success or failure will set the stage for enthusiasm or rejection of the goals of education established at the higher grade levels. Ideally, each pupil entering the intermediate grades or middle school (grades 4, 5, 6 or 7) should have become proficient in a number of basic skills essential for progress in reading, writing, talking or computation. These skills are the basis for proficiency in a number of fields, like social studies, the sciences or languages. The content may be specialized, but the approach to mastering the new subject matter should be basically the same. Boys and girls must be ready to look for clues, ideas and hidden meanings; when reading, they must begin to react to the author's purpose in the light of their own experiences and for the first time begin to evaluate what they see or hear. If the answers to questions are not available in a given source, they must be prepared to seek them elsewhere. It is this latter ability that often distinguishes the gifted and talented pupil from those with less ability. Teachers should encourage these students to learn the meaning of research and independent study. They should not be kept waiting while the slower students complete the required assignment.

2 Techniques of Identification

Practice teachers often leave a classroom after a period of observation with a disappointed look or comment such as "Those gifted kids—where are they?" or "I didn't see any oddballs. Why, these boys and girls act normal" or "I heard that Joey was a smart kid, but he didn't know the answer to a fairly simple question."

These college students are like many teachers and laymen who have the mistaken idea that it is easy to identify gifted and talented youngsters in or out of the classroom. There *are* some rare exceptions who will stand out in any gathering, but others look and act so natural that the untrained observer will refuse to acknowledge their existence even when the evidence is placed clearly before him. This is what makes the problem of education so difficult. People look for stereotypes that may be nonexistent except in their own minds. Other adults may see signs of giftedness but are not able to translate their awareness into positive action on behalf of the gifted pupil who would benefit from a modified curriculum.

Many parents want to know if their kindergarten children are gifted. Sometimes the trained teacher or school psychologist may single out with ease individual five-year-olds who are socially, emotionally and mentally far more mature than their chronological years would indicate; however, other potentially gifted children may not show any outward signs of giftedness until they begin to face up to the challenges of a formal reading, arithmetic or writing program. The school environment may bring out strengths that were obscured by a limited home environment. On the other hand, the school curriculum may be so limited or narrow that talent, special interest or leadership qualities are never given a chance to develop or expand. As each pupil progresses through school, the teachers have a responsibility to continue to search for signs of superior talent or for intellectual maturity far above the average.

Giftedness Revealed in Different Ways

The range of intelligence for gifted children may be such that it would be difficult to conceive of placing a number of such students in the same classroom with any expectation that they would be even closely homogeneous in their interests and abilities. One pupil may have an IQ in the low 160's; a second pupil may have an IQ in the 130 to 140 range; and a third pupil's IQ may approach 180. But home and school environments may fail to recognize differences in their physical, emotional, social and language development patterns. The mere fact that the three pupils have exceptionally high intelligence quotients is not enough. One of the students appears to be tone-deaf and has no interest in music whereas a second individual shows a keen interest in playing several musical instruments. The first two may have an unquenchable thirst for knowledge about the world of science, but the third pupil would much rather devote his free time to writing poetry and short stories than worry about scientific experiments. Individual differences among the potentially talented or gifted can frustrate any specially gifted class teacher who wants to establish a program based upon the pupils' needs.

Some educators refuse to recognize pupils with intelligence quotients below 130 as belonging to the gifted classification. They see a need to limit the range and thereby bring about a form of homogeneity in at least one recognizable trait, namely, mental maturity. Other educators insist that pupils with special talents be included in the classification. The creative factor confuses the issue because creativity can be associated with the pupil having an IQ of 118 as well as the one having an IQ of 155. The artist, the musician, the mechanically minded person, the literary expert and the mathematician have their place in the educational world. Some of them need little outside assistance to find themselves, but others need experiences before they can begin to demonstrate their ability in one or more highly specialized fields of endeavor. Creativity is something that must be nurtured; therefore, the teacher in the regular classroom or in the special class for the highly gifted must be prepared to guide and encourage the individual who has demonstrated high interests or special abilities. In many classrooms these signs may not reveal themselves unless the learning environment is conducive to the birth and growth of ideas, to the encouragement of the curious to seek out answers to their questions, and to the development of leadership qualities.

The average learner and the gifted or talented will have many common needs and interests. These can become the basis for a rich and varied educational program, but normal achievement ranges may be far too low to expect the full maturation of potentially gifted pupils. This is where the concept of non-gradedness or the special class for the gifted becomes a challenge to the educator. He must be ready to accelerate or broaden the learning experiences of boys and girls who show that they can act or think independently or with little adult assistance. At times he may have to provide them with motivation and guidance, but for the most part he has to create a learning environment *flexible* enough to allow for the growth and development of a wide range of superior accomplishments in both academic and non-academic fields.

Individual Intelligence Tests

School psychologists generally elect to use individual tests like the Stanford-Binet Intelligence Scale or the Wechsler Intelligence Scale for Children to measure the mental capacities of pupils referred to them for study. The results of both test series can be used to predict what individual pupils may do in the academic world of tomorrow. However, some authorities consider the Stanford-Binet Scale more suitable than the Wechsler Intelligence Scale for use with pre-first grade children. Since both tests require special training on the part of the examiner, the very small school system will often not have the services of a professional staff member capable of administering and evaluating one of these tests. In addition, the administration, scoring or interpretation of test results is such a time-consuming task that the number of pupils who can be given an individual examination of mental ability is limited. For this reason, each school system may establish a priority list of students for special examination.

In many school systems group intelligence tests are used to identify potentially gifted pupils because of the time and cost factors. Most of the schools lack personnel to carry out a long-range testing program that will give them an individual IQ for each pupil, but some school principals try to have all the children in at least one grade tested with the Binet or Wechsler scale. Unfortunately, this practice tends to give only one indication of intellectual giftedness. Time and money are generally not available for one or more follow-up tests at upper age or grade levels. For example, School M makes it a practice to have a Stanford-Binet administered to each child while he is in kindergarten or first grade. School S tries to acquire an individual test score for each pupil in the fourth grade. School P limits the psychologist's time to pupils who have academic or emotional problems. School C uses many other tests and records to screen out the potentially gifted. The names of selected students are then forwarded to the psychologist for supporting evidence that a pupil is intellectually gifted.

Group Intelligence Tests as a Screening Device

Parents and teachers rely heavily upon the IQ as an indication that a particular child or group of children belongs in the intellectually gifted category. Unfortunately many of them are prone to place too much emphasis upon a single test score. There are many factors that can influence the results of any test; therefore, each school should adopt a testing schedule that over a number of years will provide the members of the teaching staff with several intelligence test ratings for each pupil. The test schedule for one school system calls for group intelligence testing in grades one, three, five, seven and nine. While this seems like an excessive number of tests to administer, the multiplicity of test scores can serve as a check against an individual's longitudinal mental growth pattern. Some other school systems wait until pupils reach the third grade to institute a testing program, but this can leave first, second and starting third grade teachers with little data about children's mental ability to support or refute their own observations.

The group intelligence test should be considered as one of several factors indicating giftedness. From such a test the observer may identify several kinds of mental abilities such as spatial relationships, verbal concepts, numerical reasoning or logical reasoning. As a rule, group intelligence tests will not show the same high intelligence range as can be obtained on the Stanford-Binet Intelligence Test. Also, the variations in the top or maximum scores of group tests may warrant special individualized tests for pupils rated as having an intelligence quotient of 125 or above. Some group intelligence tests may give two types of IQ's. For example, the California Short-Form Test of Mental Maturity provides a language IQ and a non-language IQ. The latter index is generally considered more reliable than the verbal IQ when one is dealing with children from low cultural backgrounds or when a study is being made of the mental abilities of children having only recently begun to learn the English language. Boys and girls who excel in reading may show much higher scores on the verbal section of such tests than they do on the nonverbal sections. In cases where the range between the scores of group and individual tests is excessive, further testing may be desired in order to obtain a more refined intelligence test score.

Types of Group Intelligence Tests

If a school system lacks a systematic testing program it is recommended that a group test be selected that can be administered at every grade level of the elementary and junior high school. This will require different test forms for different-aged children. Some of the following tests may serve as a screening device:

Test	Age-Grade Range	Publisher
California Short-Form Test of Mental Maturity	Kindergarten to adults	California Test Bureau
Cooperative School and College Ability Tests (SCAT)	Grades 4 to 14	Educational Testing Service
Davis-Eells Test of General Intelligence	Grades 1 to 6	Harcourt, Brace & World, Inc.
Henmon-Nelson Tests of Mental Ability; Revised Edition	Grades 3 to 12 and college	Houghton Mifflin Co.
Kuhlmann-Anderson Intelligence Tests	Grades K to 12	Personnel Press
Kuhlmann-Finch Intelligence Tests	Grades 1 to 12	Personnel Press

Test	Age-Grade Range	Publisher
Lorge-Thorndike Intelligence Tests	Grades K to 12	Houghton Mifflin Co.
Otis Quick Scoring Mental Ability Tests	Grades 1 to 16	Harcourt, Brace & World, Inc.
Pintner General Ability Tests	Grades K to 12	Harcourt, Brace & World, Inc.
SRA Tests of Educational Ability	Grades K to 12	Science Research Associates
Terman-McNemar Test of Mental Ability	Grades 7 to 12	Harcourt, Brace & World, Inc.

After group tests have been administered and scored, teacher teams or individuals with a strong testing background may use the test data to begin to identify potentially gifted children. This is where other supporting data should be used in order to obtain a more reliable index of each pupil's intellectual ability. When achievement records, teacher reports, reading progress charts and other special qualities do not support high or low test results, further testing will be most helpful. In some schools test specialists or psychologists make it a point to administer a Wechsler intelligence test (WISC) or a Stanford-Binet intelligence test to all pupils obtaining very low or very high intelligence test scores in the original screening. In addition, they give all questionable cases the individual test to secure a more reliable measure.

The Use of Mental Age

Two pupils may both have IQ's of 127, but this does not necessarily mean that they should be achieving at the same level even when they are in the same grade. Chronological age must be considered along with the intelligence quotient before a teacher can make an estimate as to an individual's ability to work at higher achievement levels. This is one reason why teachers are advised to consider mental age instead of intelligence quotients when trying to predict where children should be in a given subject. The M.A. or mental age refers to the performance level of a pupil who has taken an intelligence test. Mental maturity is expressed in years and months and is based on the fact that the individual made a raw score equal to that of a typical person of that chronological age level. Thus, a nine-year-old who is said to have an M.A. of 10–6 is conceivably performing at the same rate as a typical person in the initial testing sample who had a chronological age of 10–6.

If teachers list pupils according to mental age, they can anticipate what each individual may do in terms of so-called grade standards. For example, the pupil who has an M.A. of 10–6 may be expected to read on a fifth grade level. Table 2 is designated as a mental age conversion table. The classroom teacher can use it to compare standardized test results with potential expectancy levels for reported mental ages. Actually, a rough measure can be obtained merely by subtracting five from the M.A. to obtain the expected class achievement. (Teachers should remember that a single achievement test score may indicate an actual instructional level that is at least one-half year below a given grade equivalent.)

Mental age can be used as an indicator of an individual's ability to succeed in most academic subjects. However, since it is based upon factors that measure abstract intelligence, it does not indicate how the pupil will learn in situations calling for a different type of intelligence such as social intelligence, mechanical ability, musical ability or artistic ability. The mental age of the individual will increase from year to year with chronological age at a rate commensurate with the pupil's intelligence. As a rule, tests given at early chronological ages tend to be less reliable than those given at later ages, but an IQ obtained at age eight or nine will show a very high correlation with one obtained at ages fourteen, fifteen or sixteen.

Table 2 MENTAL AGE-GRADE CONVERSION TABLE

Mental Age	*Reading Grade	Mental Age	Reading Grade	Mental Age	Reading Grade	Mental Age	Reading Grade
		10-0	4.7	14-0	8.7	18-0	12.8
		10-1	4.7	14-1	8.8	18-1	12.8
6-2	1.0	10-2	4.8	14-2	8.9	18-2	12.9
6-3	1.1	10-3	4.9	14-3	8.9	18-3	13.0
6-4	1.2	10-4	5.0	14-4	9.0	18-4	13.0
6-5	1.3	10-5	5.1	14-5	9.1	18-5	13.1
6-6	1.3	10-6	5.2	14-6	9.2	18-6	13.2
6-7	1.4	10-7	5.2	14-7	9.3	18-7	13.2
6-8	1.5	10-8	5.3	14-8	9.4	18-8	13.3
6-9	1.6	10-9	5.3	14-9	9.4	18-9	13.4
6-10	1.7	10-10	5.4	14-10	9.5	18-10	13.5
6-11	1.7	10-11	5.5	14-11	9.6	18-11	13.6
7-0	1.8	11-0	5.6	15-0	9.7	19-0	13.7
7-1	1.9	11-1	5.7	15-1	9.8	19-1	13.8
7-2	2.0	11-2	5.8	15-2	9.9	19-2	13.9
7-3	2.0	11-3	5.8	15-3	9.9	19-3	14.0
7-4	2.1	11-4	5.9	15-4	10.0	19-4	14.1
7-5	2.2	11-5	6.0	15-5	10.1	19-5	14.2
7-6	2.3	11-6	6.1	15-6	10.2	19-6	14.3
7-7	2.4	11-7	6.2	15-7	10.3	19-7	14.4
7-8	2.5	11-8	6.3	15-8	10.4	19-8	14.5
7-9	2.5	11-9	6.3	15-9	10.5	19-9	14.6
7-10	2.6	11-10	6.4	15-10	10.6	19-10	14.7
7-11	2.7	11-11	6.5	15-11	10.6	19-11	14.8
8-0	2.8	12-0	6.6	16-0	10.7	20-0	14.9
8-1	2.8	12-1	6.7	16-1	10.7	20-1	15.0
8-2	2.9	12-2	6.8	16-2	10.8	20-2	15.1
8-3	3.0	12-3	6.8	16-3	10.8	20-3	15.2
8-4	3.1	12-4	6.9	16-4	10.9	20-4	15.3
8-5	3.1	12-5	7.0	16-5	10.9	20-5	15.4
8-6	3.2	12-6	7.1	16-6	11.0	20-6	15.5
8-7	3.3	12-7	7.2	16-7	11.1	20-7	15.6
8-8	3.4	12-8	7.3	16-8	11.2	20-8	15.7
8-9	3.5	12-9	7.3	16-9	11.3	20-9	15.8
8-10	3.6	12-10	7.4	16-10	11.4	20-10	15.9
8-11	3.6	12-11	7.5	16-11	11.5	20-11	16.1
9-0	3.7	13-0	7.6	17-0	11.6	21-0	16.2
9-1	3.8	13-1	7.7	17-1	11.7	21-1	16.3
9-2	3.9	13-2	7.8	17-2	11.8	21-2	16.4
9-3	4.0	13-3	7.9	17-3	11.8		
9-4	4.0	13-4	8.0	17-4	11.8		
9-5	4.1	13-5	8.0	17-5	12.0		
9-6	4.2	13-6	8.1	17-6	12.1		
9-7	4.3	13-7	8.2	17-7	12.1		
9-8	4.4	13-8	8.3	17-8	12.2		
9-9	4.4	13-9	8.4	17-9	12.6		
9-10	4.5	13-10	8.5	17-10	12.6		
9-11	4.6	13-11	8.6	17-11	12.7		

* NOTE: Can be used to show Reading, Arithmetic, Language grade equivalent for Mental Age. Based on averages computed from norms of Stanford Achievement Test, Iowa Every-Pupil Test, California Test of Mental Maturity—Primary Series, California Capacity Questionnaire, Gates Primary Reading Test, and Gates Reading Survey for Grades 3 to 19.

Mental age profiles can be developed that show the intellectual potential of a boy or girl. These profiles can guide the teacher, school administrator or guidance counselor in the selection of courses for a given individual. Here again the educator is warned that a single criterion may not be sufficient to identify special talents. On the other hand, the mental age profile may reveal talents that were not considered present in the pupil's makeup. A number of studies of a longitudinal nature by Armstrong and others pointed up the danger of overemphasizing the intellectual capacity of given individuals at an early age because mental growth patterns are not constant. Enough individuals have shown a sudden acceleration of mental growth to warrant continued study and retesting of pupils as they progress through the school. Thus, a boy or girl who may appear to be merely high average in intelligence when in the third grade may show a rise in mental ability to warrant reclassification as a truly gifted pupil at the seventh grade level.

Tailoring the Program to the IQ or M.A.

Many laymen have been taught to interpret scores in terms of norms for a grade. The danger in this lies in the fact that teachers become satisfied with standardized achievement test scores that approximate the grade equivalent but do not measure up to the student's capabilities. For example, a pupil taking a standardized achievement test in December and obtaining an arithmetic grade equivalency score of 6.4 may be considered to be working at a satisfactory sixth grade level for sixth graders. While this may be true for a pupil with an IQ of 100, it is not true for the pupil with an IQ of 128. The latter student has a mental age of approximately 13–3 and may be considered as having an arithmetic expectancy level on a high seventh or low eighth grade level.

In one school system the public was constantly led to believe that boys and girls were making a good showing on standardized tests because the median scores tended to be two points (.2) above a grade norm. Actual examination of intelligence test scores for the entire school system showed average grade intelligence scores approximating a norm of 120; yet pupils were lauded for obtaining achievement score medians based upon norms set for classes having an average IQ of 100. For example, the fifth grade expectancy level in reading comprehension was 6.6; therefore, teachers and parents who accepted a grade norm of 5.2 or 5.3 were being too easily satisfied. A new school principal, recognizing the danger, worked with the staff to build up basic reading comprehension skills. In two years the average class median score for reading had been raised by more than a full grade.

The curriculum of an entire class, grade, or school should be considered in terms of the ability of the pupils. Slow-learning pupils should not be expected to meet standards set for average learners. At the same time, intellectually gifted pupils should be challenged to work with materials and ideas suited to their social, emotional and mental maturity levels. The average IQ of a boy or girl, as well as that of a group of boys and girls, should be considered a guide in the establishment of curriculum standards. However, individual differences should still be recognized since pupils with the same intellectual levels can have different types of intelligence. These differences may be reflected in a class where the boys have the ability to achieve at high levels in science and mathematics whereas the girls may be achieving at average levels in these two subjects but outdoing the boys in general reading and writing activities.

In communities where pupils come from high socioeconomic levels, the entire curriculum for a whole school or even a segment of a series of classes may be enriched or broadened in order to challenge each individual to work closer to expectation levels for reported mental ages. On the other hand, the top 10 per cent of children in schools drawing from very low socioeconomic levels may be complimented if they are able to meet standard grade norms, even though there is a possibility that this entire segment of the school population may be considered potentially gifted. A school principal in such a school may find it helpful to have the Cattell Culture-Free Intelligence Test administered to determine the exact level of intelligence of the highest achieving students. The test results of such a test may help in the identification of potentially gifted pupils who, with guidance and special attention, could raise their general class achievement to better than an average performance level.

Standardized Achievement Tests as a Screening Device

In the absence of adequate intelligence test data, the teacher may look to standardized achievement test scores as a clue to potential giftedness. However, where records show one or more group or individual IQ scores, the pupil's achievement in various subject matter fields will help substantiate earlier conclusions, or the results may show up areas of strength or weakness. A boy with a high mental age and an average or below-average achievement score in arithmetic, reading or language may be classified as an underachiever. If he is working up to grade level and seems to be an individual with good work habits, the fault may lie not in the pupil but in the original intelligence test findings. In other instances low academic achievement will parallel the teacher's observation that the individual has very poor work patterns, lacks motivation, or has a poor foundation in essential skill areas such as word recognition and mastery of fundamental processes ordinarily taught at lower grade levels.

Intellectually gifted children from the average community tend to show achievement at two or more years above the grade norm. In low socioeconomic levels gifted children may not be classified as such if the teacher is looking for pupils working above normal grade expectations. She may be lucky if she has any pupils working at or about the grade norm; however, these pupils may be the ones in need of further study if their achievement is substantially above that of their peermates. In such schools the teacher may elect the top 10 per cent of an achievement test range as a possible criterion for identifying giftedness.

Types of Standardized Achievement Tests

Primary grade teachers usually limit their achievement testing to reading and arithmetic, but intermediate and upper grade teachers can find numerous standardized achievement tests available for areas of special interest. While individual subject tests can be used, the common practice is to test for achievement in several subject fields by using a test battery. Some of the tests that may serve as a screening device as well as an evaluative instrument

Test	Age-Grade Range	Publisher
California Achievement Tests	Grades 1 to 9	California Test Bureau
Iowa Test of Basic Skills	Grades 3 to 9	Houghton Mifflin Co.
Metropolitan Achievement Tests	Grades 1 to 9	Harcourt, Brace & World, Inc.
Sequential Tests of Educational Progress (STEP)	Grades 4 to 14	Educational Testing Service
SRA Achievement Tests	Grades 2 to 9	Science Research Associates
Stanford Achievement Tests	Grades 1 to 9	Harcourt, Brace & World, Inc.

are listed above. Different test forms are available for various ages and grade levels.

These standardized achievement tests represent commonly used tests. The batteries are generally limited to tests for two or three grades, but this range may not be adequate for gifted children. In many cases these pupils will receive scores far above the score considered normal for their grade. This could lead to misjudgments of their readiness for higher-level learning activities. Retesting with the next-higher-level test battery will often show achievement that is much closer to actual class performance.

At the high school level the following tests may be helpful:

Test	Age-Grade Range	Publisher
California Achievement Tests	Grades 9 to 14	California Test Bureau
Cooperative General Achievement Tests	Grades 10 to 12	Educational Testing Service
Essential High School Content Battery	Grades 9 to 13	Harcourt, Brace & World, Inc.
The Iowa Tests of Educational Development	Grades 8 to 13	Science Research Associates
Sequential Tests of Educational Development	Grades 10 to 14	Cooperative Test Division, Educational Testing Service

The standardized achievement test can be administered at different times during a school year, but many school systems test in the fall, at midyear or at the end of the school year. Although not all achievement tests are diagnostic instruments, teachers can use some of them to identify basic areas of weakness which can then become the basis for concentrated teaching or study during the remainder of the term.

Limitations of Group Tests

Both group intelligence and achievement tests are essential screening devices for the identification of gifted pupils, but they will not provide the evidence teachers are seeking when boys and girls have serious reading problems. In too many cases poor reading is associated with low intelligence or limited ability. Unfortunately, this is not always true. A large number of poor readers have extremely high IQ's, but this will not be evident to the observer who depends upon tests that have a reading base.

Boys and girls with high emotional problems may fail to register very high on group intelligence or achievement tests. Emotional imbalance may interfere with the development of the work patterns needed to make a good showing in regular classroom activities or in the test situation. In some cases lack of motivation may be the factor that limits an individual from revealing his true potential. Sometimes the lack of motivation may reflect poor physical health. Thus, a very bright girl had no staying power because she lacked the physical strength to work for any sustained period of time. As a result, her test results were always low because she failed to complete tests or subdivisions of the tests.

Standardized tests do not measure the same things; therefore, it becomes impossible to compare the results of two different achievement tests or intelligence tests. Similarly, test results on some achievement tests become meaningless when a low ceiling on a given test or subdivision results in an interpolated score for the brighter pupils. This may lead an individual to expect too much from a boy or girl. On the opposite side of the picture is the low ceiling on many group intelligence tests. Cases have been reported repeatedly of students being only moderately gifted who, upon further testing with individual tests, were found to be highly gifted. The danger of the low ceiling on group intelligence tests lies in the underestimation of the true potential of gifted children.

Other Types of Tests for Identifying Gifted Children

The group intelligence test and the standardized achievement test should be used to complement each other in the identification of gifted children. Though not perfect, these tests should hold a very high place in the selection of individuals for gifted programs or for the identification of special needs of a group of youngsters. In addition teachers will find the following less commonly used tests helpful.

1. *Tests to Measure Creativity.* For many years creativity was considered in terms of intelligence. An individual had to possess qualities measured on a particular test. Today, research has made it clear that the standard intelligence test does not measure traits associated with creativity. A number of approaches have been made to the problem of identifying creativity. Guilford's studies have led to the development of tests that attempt to identify the factors associated with high divergent thinking. Users of the Guilford-type tests have come to the conclusion that the correlation between intelligence and creativity tends to be low. Intellectually gifted children may be creative, but not all creative children have the high intelligence associated with the word gifted.

In searching for elements associated with creativity, research workers are stressing the importance of fluency of response, flexibility, originality of responses and the ability to evaluate. Since teachers can help children improve these qualities, Torrance and others see creativity as something that can be trained. His developmental curves on the growth of divergent thinking reveal, however, that cultural influences affect the degree to which an individual can be trained to be creative. However, while the schools may have as their goal the development of creativity, teachers tend to show preference for the conformist pupil over the non-conforming one. And in a number of studies of tests designed to show the relationship of personality to creativity, it is usually the non-conforming students who show the most creative tendencies.

Another problem in using tests to measure creativity is the fact that individual students may express their creative spirit in different ways. Therefore, the correlation between various subdivisions of a test for creativity may be very low. This would appear to be especially true where individuals show a preference for work in a field of art instead of science, but again there is the danger that family background and cultural patterns may give a distorted picture of the true ability of the potentially talented youngster.

No single test can be recommended to measure creativity, but there may be a breakthrough in the near future. Experiments are being made with new types of tests which attempt to measure multiple facets of intelligence. The standard intelligence and achievement tests can be used to help identify high achievers and pupils with above average intelligence, but neither test alone or combined will point out the creative individual. Further study of personality factors and actual achievement in specialized fields may help teachers in their attempt to identify creative children.

2. *Aptitude Tests.* Most teachers are more familiar with general intelligence tests than they are with tests that attempt to measure specialized aptitudes. Guidance counselors are familiar with such tests, which attempt to measure vocational aptitudes. One commonly used test is the Differential Aptitude Test Battery prepared by the Psychological Corporation. It attempts to measure different types of abilities through eight subtests, namely, (a) verbal reasoning, (b) numerical ability, (c) abstract reasoning, (d) space relationship, (e) mechanical reasoning, (f) clerical speed and accuracy, (g) language usage, sentences and (h) language usage, spelling. Other tests of this type are the General Aptitude Test Battery and the Flanagan Aptitude Classification Test Battery.

The Chicago Test of Primary Mental Abilities, prepared

by Science Research Associates, is highly recommended for use with gifted pupils at or above the fifth grade level since it attempts to measure specific types of intelligence. Pupils taking this test may reveal exceptionally high abilities on one or more of the following subtests which measure (a) number, (b) verbal meaning, (c) space, (d) word fluency, (e) reasoning and (f) memory. Thus, a low total score could still point out the student who has a potential for giftedness through a special type of intelligence.

3. *Reading Tests.* Numerous reading tests are available for students at all educational levels. While the average test battery measures some phases of reading, special reading tests have value in that they measure aspects of reading that are not evident in the ordinary achievement test battery. Some of them become excellent diagnostic instruments because they show areas of special skill or weakness. Teachers will find the following tests helpful.

Test	*Age-Grade Range*	*Publisher*
Durrell-Sullivan Reading Capacity and Achievement Tests	Grades 2 to 6	Harcourt, Brace & World, Inc.
Gates Primary Reading Tests	Grades 1 and 2	Bureau of Publications, Teachers College, Columbia University
Gates Advanced Primary Reading Tests	Grades 2 and 3	
Gates Basic Reading Tests	Grades 3 to 8	
Iowa Silent Reading Test	Grades 4 to 13	Harcourt, Brace & World, Inc.
Traxler High School Reading Test	Grades 10 to 12	Public School Publishing Co.
Neson-Denny Reading Test	Grades 9 to 12	Houghton Mifflin Co.

4. *Prognostic Tests.* A number of tests have been developed in an attempt to predict the possibility of success in arithmetic, algebra, geometry, shorthand, foreign languages and other academic subjects. One of the most

widely used of these prognostic tests is the reading readiness test (Metropolitan, Gates, Lee-Clark, Murphey-Durrell). This test may have general appeal for those who are trying to identify giftedness at an early age. The reading readiness test is often given in kindergarten or at the beginning of first grade in an attempt to guide teachers in the formation of reading or number groups. Used discriminatingly with other data the reading readiness test can be considered an instrument to identify pupils who have reached a high level of language development. The authors recommend the use of such tests on a broad experimental basis before entry into school to modify entrance age into school for gifted and nongifted children or to assign young children to teachers who can plan special activities for them in terms of strengths and weaknesses.

The reading readiness test has much in common with an intelligence test. Both depend upon the use of test questions calling for the knowledge of word meanings as well as the ability to perceive likenesses and differences; but the reading readiness test usually stresses the skills considered necessary for formal reading. The use of both tests can be helpful with chronologically young children, but predictions of potential giftedness should be limited to a short period of time. There is always the danger that early environmental factors may lead one to classify as gifted those children who with time, experience and the leveling activities of the school will end up merely as children with high average potential and good work-study patterns. Thus, intelligence and actual achievement will be decisive elements for a later and more refined prognosis of giftedness.

5. *Special Aptitude Tests.* Batteries of tests have been developed in an attempt to select boys and girls for special training in law, medicine, engineering, nursing and accounting. These special aptitude tests may be of little interest at lower elementary or junior high school grade levels; however, the more specialized music and art aptitude tests may be considered measures of potential

giftedness in the creative arts. The Seashore Measures of Musical Talent are often used to measure musical aptitude but there is still considerable disagreement about the reliability or validity of the tests as *real* measures of creative talent in the field of music.

Numerous tests exist to measure aptitude for art, but the argument is frequently raised that they are really art achievement tests. As such, they may help predict success in the field of art, but environmental factors could influence the results. True creativity in the fine arts fields may not be discovered if boys and girls have never had much, if any, so-called art experiences. However, some of these tests have shown a good correlation between the prognosis of success in art and later accomplishment. The following art tests may be used to measure aptitude for work in art:

    a)   The Meier Art Judgment Test
    b)   The Graves Design Judgment Test
    c)   The Horn Art Aptitude Inventory
    d)   The Lewerenz Tests in Fundamental Abilities of Visual Art
    e)   The Knauber Art Ability Test
    f)   The Lewerenz Fundamental Art Abilities Test

Some school systems have eliminated formal art tests in favor of having a screening committee review samples of the creative art work completed by boys and girls under the guidance of their teachers. These work samples are more apt to be valuable indications of creative art interest and ability than are some of the more formal or standardized art tests.

6. *The Interest Inventory.* The average teacher knows less about the interest inventory or the personality test than about achievement or intelligence tests. Moreover, parents know very little about such tests. As a result, parents get excited about the kind of questions that are asked on the tests. These questions attempt to identify interests and characteristics of behavior that will help the teacher or guidance counselor understand the pupil as a person. This information could be most helpful in work-

ing with gifted pupils because interest is a strong motivating force that could be used to establish special class or study groups on the basis of common interests.

On the other hand, since these tests are not based upon achievement or ability, the fact that the individual shows apparent interest in science, mathematics, music or business is no guarantee that the pupil will be successful in these areas. Some of the best work in the field of interest surveys has been done in vocational areas. Tests like the Strong Vocational Interest Blank or the Kuder Preference Record have been more valuable instruments with older high school and college students than they have been with upper elementary or junior high school students. These tests attempt to identify the interests associated with specific vocations. Unfortunately, there is always a danger that interests can be faked. This will be especially true of bright and gifted pupils who have the ability to anticipate what the teacher or author wants. Results of such tests should be considered a part of a complete testing program supplemented by teacher observation, anecdotal records, biographic studies and parent reports.

7. *The Personality Tests.* Most pupils, especially the brighter ones, enjoy taking personality tests. Some of them may even take delight in the chance to create a personality that is much different from the one they actually possess. But tests like the Minnesota Multiphasic Personality Test have built-in safeguards against those who would deliberately or unconsciously withhold information, particularly in the case of teen-agers who may be reluctant to let others, especially teachers, know their true feelings.

A large number of tests have been developed to identify the temperament or personality of individual students. These tests can give the trained examiner valuable information about behavior characteristics of potentially gifted pupils. For example, a high score under the category *general activity* of the Guilford-Zimmerman Temperament Survey may indicate a rapid pace of activities: energy, vitality; keeping in motion; production, efficiency, liking for speed; hurrying; quickness of action; enthusiasm, liveliness. A teacher's observations may support the reliability of the test finding, and the examiner may, therefore, feel safe in making recommendations that call for speed, energy and enthusiasm. Teachers using the Mooney Problem Check List or the SRA Junior Inventory and Youth Inventory may find that pupils have listed problems that can become the basis for further study with individuals or with groups of boys and girls having similar problems.

Teacher Marks to Help Identify the Gifted

Teacher marks are often reported as one criterion used to identify potentially gifted children, but surveys of such practices show that they are seldom used alone. In general, they are considered with IQ's, achievement test results and teacher opinion. When all are used as a composite, many of the dangers associated with subjective marking are avoided.

While recommended practice calls for early identification of the gifted, many school systems are unable to pick out the potentially gifted or talented pupils until they reach grades 4, 5 and 6, by which time sufficient data can be accumulated to present a good case for accepting or rejecting many of the names submitted as potentially talented. If good cumulative records have been kept, grade scores, IQ ranges and achievement test scores can be translated into a common denominator that when added together will give an average or giftedness rating. Since intelligence ratings and the results of standardized achievement tests are usually given high priority in the prediction of future success with high level work, teacher marks may be given less consideration. Instead of being counted on an equal basis, they may be counted as a fifth of a composite score.

Teacher marks at the primary grade level are apt to be directly related to a pupil's success in reading because teachers at the first and second grade levels devote the major portion of their time and effort to language development activities centering about reading, writing and speaking. These teachers do not devote much time to formal subject testing, so marks at these lower grade levels have no real value. A better criterion would be the *pupil's level of accomplishment in the basic reading series.* Unfortunately, the reluctance of the average teacher to introduce gifted pupils or rapid learners to advanced-level basic readers by the middle of the school year could negate the value of using actual reading accomplishment or report card grades as valid criteria for measuring giftedness. In a truly nongraded program many potentially gifted children would reveal their potential by moving through the basic primary reading program in two years instead of three. Also, in such a program there is a possibility that some of the more gifted boys and girls would have an opportunity to reach new and higher levels of classroom achievement in arithmetic. However, this would become evident only when teachers introduced subgrouping on a wider scale than they usually do for arithmetic activities.

Intermediate grade teacher marks should compare with the scores made on actual standardized subject tests. Where teacher marks and test scores are comparable, actual accomplishment may be accepted as a criterion of potential giftedness. It is when there is a wide discrepancy between the two measures that the investigator should attempt to find more supporting evidence. For example, was the pupil consistently above grade on other standardized tests? Has he been getting poor marks for the past two, three or four years in a subject like reading? If this should be true, the next step would be an informal reading test by an unbiased teacher to determine how successfully the pupil can read standard reading textbooks. The very fact that there is a low correlation between teacher marks and the achievement test scores may be considered sufficient proof that something is wrong, that the current program is not meeting the basic needs of the student. In such cases the introduction of information other than the IQ may help in the identification process. For example, the opinion ratings of teachers, scout leaders, religious leaders, social workers and others who know the individual's work patterns, interests or leadership potential may shed light upon the type of performance that can be expected of a pupil who is considered potentially gifted.

Marks have different meanings to various teachers, parents and school administrators. Unfortunately, teacher marks are not made on the basis of a common yardstick or standard. An *A* will not always mean the same to the teachers from several grades or subject fields of a given school system. These differences in grading practices will increase as marks are compiled from a number of school systems. Thus, pupils who transfer from one community to another may find that marks are not comparable. If marks are to be used as a unit of measurement, those marks given to pupils placed in heterogeneous classes should have greater significance than those given to pupils in homogeneous classes. Some schools have adopted a marking code that guarantees the receipt of minimum grades for pupils assigned to advanced-level courses or learning activities, but there is evidence that only a very small number of school systems follow this practice. For example, eighth grade pupils are placed in advanced-level science classes with the understanding that no student will receive a mark less than an *A* or *B*. Or a twelfth grade pupil takes an Honors course in English. Because he is competing with outstanding students, he is shocked to receive his first *D* or *F*. Does the college know that the *D* would have been an *A* in the regular English course? If so, will he receive recognition when the *D* places the applicant for admission below the cut-off point for acceptance?

This mixed marking philosophy can interfere with the identification of gifted pupils because some pupils at

upper grade levels learn to conserve their strength and
energy by following the crowd. It may be much easier to
obtain an *A* average by selecting so-called soft courses or
by not giving in to the pressures to take advanced-level
courses. In this case low pupil marks may have their
parallel in a lower achievement range on standardized
tests.

Marks should have little significance in a truly nongraded school. The evidence of potential giftedness will
often lie in actual achievement in class and on standardized achievement tests. Academic progress may be somewhat slower among disadvantaged boys and girls than
among those of children not culturally disadvantaged.
Here giftedness may be considered a buried element
waiting to be uncovered if and when the top 10 per cent
of a class or school is considered worthy of special
attention.

Progress Charts

In some schools the classroom teacher keeps a record of
pupil progress in the classroom. Teachers may find that
the boys and girls who find success rapidly in day-by-day
learning activities have characteristics associated with
giftedness. For example, a reading chart may indicate
how fast students progress from one reading level to the
next. Thus, a reading time line may show that some
pupils have little need for early reading readiness materials. Furthermore, their progress through the preprimers
and the primer and first reader may be steady and rapid,
so there would be little need to maintain a constant review
of basic vocabulary or special reading skills. The pupils
may be ready to move into higher-level reading skills
without the use of numerous supplemental books. In the
middle grades they may show that skills are mastered
quickly in reading, arithmetic and social studies; and by
the time they reach the upper grades, the pupils may show

a record of wide reading experiences in literature, science and social studies fields.

Progress records may supplement the cumulative record. A check list for basic arithmetic skills encompassing the actual achievements in class over several years will often help guide the teacher in directing students to new and challenging higher-level experiences. The record of library skills or work-study skills may tell a teacher whether or not an individual is ready to do high-level free-lance work with sixth, seventh or eighth grade materials. A chronology of a pupil's achievements in art may be revealed in the study of a folder containing samples of creative work done by him at different age or grade levels. An accumulation of creative writing papers may reveal evidences of talent not always discerned in a single composition. A record of the books read in and out of class may indicate areas of special interest, as well as high-level reading achievement. The pupil's spelling list may show the mastery of a basic vocabulary at an early age. This record, plus a study of the pupil's oral and written vocabulary, may point out the individual who is performing well above normal age or grade standards.

A study of progress records may reveal areas of weakness as well as of strength. For example, one individual may show a history of poor muscular coordination. This may be reflected in his failure to develop skill in writing, art or athletics. Another bright pupil may reveal himself as a slow but methodical worker. This could put him at a disadvantage in the constant search for broadening experiences. Many bright high school pupils flounder because nobody checked their rate of reading or their level of comprehension or took the time to do something constructive to remedy their handicap.

A record of progress in this case could supplement the story told by achievement tests. Known areas of strength or weakness could become focal points for emphasis. For example, Harry had an IQ of 132, but his classwork showed low achievement. A tenth grade teacher studied Harry's reading progress chart and found the boy seldom completed a library book. In search of a reason, the teacher discovered that the boy was reading about 125 words a minute instead of an expected 300 or more words a minute.

Similarly, Nancy was doing poorly in arithmetic until an eighth grade teacher studied the cumulative records and found several anecdotal notes describing early emotional upsets over arithmetic assignments. A further study of her standard achievement test grade equivalents showed superior achievement in every major subject field except arithmetic. An arithmetic inventory test showed weakness in simple fundamental processes. Nancy's need was review and reteaching in these areas, so a special time schedule was developed to free the girl from language art activities in order to give her time to strengthen her arithmetic background.

The following notations on a progress record chart indicated an area of interest that could be cultivated.

"Terry brought in a huge hornet's nest for sharing time." Grade 1

"Terry entertained the class with interesting bird calls." Grade 2

"Terry's bird collection fascinated the class." Grade 3

"Terry took an injured bird home today." Grade 4

"Terry's art portfolio contains sketches and drawings of birds that are so realistic that one would believe they had been copied if we had not seen his skill with brush, pencil, and crayon." Grade 8

Progress records may be formal or informal—a teacher may merely jot down notes on scraps of paper or she may note progress on a printed cumulative check list that goes from one teacher to the next. Teachers may be asked to indicate one outstanding achievement during a marking period. This may be recorded on a duplicate report card and the cumulative record card. These notations may be eliminated after two or three years, but in other situations they may be saved indefinitely for analysis by future teachers, guidance counselors, psychologists or school administrators.

Teacher Opinion to Supplement Data from Cumulative Records

The experienced teacher will observe the behavior of boys and girls under many types of conditions. She sees them when they are subjected to frustrating experiences like test situations, as well as when they are enthusiastic or excited. Her observations and conclusions may not always be in accord with other evidence; however, when they are positive and support the conclusion that a given student has gifted characteristics, there is a good likelihood that the pupil may fall into the superior category. When she is unwilling to accept the weight of other criteria, her judgment should be considered carefully, but not finally. If her observations are sound, it will be helpful to review the basis of her conclusions and the data taken from test records or cumulative records.

A number of studies have been made that tend to minimize the significance of teacher observations unless steps have been taken to help teachers identify characteristics associated with giftedness or talent. One approach calls for the use of guidelines or check lists such as the one shown in Table 3. This particular check list may be used for group appraisal after teachers have filled in one or both parts of the form. If cumulative records are complete the team may prefer not to use Part I. They should complete Part II, however, with the understanding that many gifted pupils may not receive a superior or 4 rating for each statement.

The conclusions based upon a check list such as Part II may support or refute conclusions based upon the data shown on Part I. If the discrepancies are heavy, the team may seek other information. For example, observations by the school nurse, the school psychologist, special subject teachers and other professional staff members may be given serious consideration. Again, observations by teachers who have worked with children at lower grade levels will prove helpful.

Table 3 A CHECK LIST TO AID IN THE IDENTIFICATION
OF GIFTED AND TALENTED STUDENTS

Part I GENERAL BACKGROUND INFORMATION

Pupil's Name _____ Grade _____ C.A. _____

Mental Ability, as Indicated by Standardized Tests

Name of Test	Date of Testing	Verbal IQ	Non-Verbal IQ	Average IQ
_____	_____	_____	_____	_____
_____	_____	_____	_____	_____
_____	_____	_____	_____	_____

General Achievement, as Indicated by Standardized Tests

	Name of Test	Date of Testing	Grade Equivalent	Percentile Rank

Reading
  Vocabulary
  Comprehension

Arithmetic
  Fundamentals
  Problems

Language
  Areas of strength

    _____
    _____

Work Study Skills
  Areas of strength

    _____
    _____

Other Special Subject Fields

    _____
    _____

Achievement in Class, Based on Teacher Observations

Reading Progress
  Is reading successfully in the top ( ) middle ( ) low ( ) group
  May be considered in the top 10 ( ) 20 ( ) 30 ( ) per cent of
  the class.

Arithmetic Progress
  Is working successfully in the top ( ) middle ( ) low ( ) group
  If children are not grouped for arithmetic, rank the pupil in
  terms of his position in class for:
    Arithmetic accuracy   top 10 ( ) 20 ( ) 30 ( ) per cent

Skill in
Fundamental Processes   top 10 ( ) 20 ( ) 30 ( ) per cent
Ability to
Solve Problems   top 10 ( ) 20 ( ) 30 ( ) per cent
Other Areas Where
Outstanding
_____ top 10 ( ) 20 ( ) 30 ( ) per cent
_____ top 10 ( ) 20 ( ) 30 ( ) per cent

Language Skill, based on teacher observation

Rank in Class

Oral Language   top 10 ( ) 15 ( ) 20 ( ) 25 ( ) per cent
Written Language   top 10 ( ) 15 ( ) 20 ( ) 25 ( ) per cent
Sentence Structure top 10 ( ) 15 ( ) 20 ( ) 25 ( ) per cent
Paragraphing Skill top 10 ( ) 15 ( ) 20 ( ) 25 ( ) per cent
Skill in Choice
of Words   top 10 ( ) 15 ( ) 20 ( ) 25 ( ) per cent
Listening Skill   top 10 ( ) 15 ( ) 20 ( ) 25 ( ) per cent

Writing Skill or Penmanship
Readability of Work   good ( ) fair ( ) poor ( )
Skill in Letter Formation   good ( ) fair ( ) poor ( )
Speed or Ease in Writing   good ( ) fair ( ) poor ( )

*Other Subjects in Which Pupil Shows Outstanding Skill or
Interest:*
Social studies   top 10 ( ) 20 ( ) 30 ( ) per cent
Science   top 10 ( ) 20 ( ) 30 ( ) per cent
Foreign language   top 10 ( ) 20 ( ) 30 ( ) per cent
Art   top 10 ( ) 20 ( ) 30 ( ) per cent
Music   top 10 ( ) 20 ( ) 30 ( ) per cent
Physical education   top 10 ( ) 20 ( ) 30 ( ) per cent
_____ top 10 ( ) 20 ( ) 30 ( ) per cent
_____ top 10 ( ) 20 ( ) 30 ( ) per cent

Parental Background
Father's Occupation _____
Highest Level of Edu-
cation Completed   Elementary ( ) Secondary ( ) College ( )
Mother's
Occupation _____
Highest Level of Edu-
cation Completed   Elementary ( ) Secondary ( ) College ( )

*Area in Which Pupil May Be Considered as Having More Than
Usual Skill or Talent for His Age or Grade*
Music: instrumental ( ) vocal ( )
Art: drawing ( ) painting ( ) other _____ ( )
Mechanical aptitude ( )

Writing ( )
Athletics ( )
Leadership skill: in class ( ) on the playground ( )
Mathematics ( )
Science ( )
Other _____ ( )

Part II GENERAL CHARACTERISTICS

Nature of Skill or Characteristic	low	average	high	superior
1. Attention span, ability to work for a prolonged period without losing interest	( )	( )	( )	( )
2. Ability to work independently (with minimum assistance from teacher or others in class)	( )	( )	( )	( )
3. Ability to assume responsibility	( )	( )	( )	( )
4. Sense of humor	( )	( )	( )	( )
5. Ability to anticipate, skill in sensing what may happen in a story, experiment, game	( )	( )	( )	( )
6. Ability to see and correct his own mistakes	( )	( )	( )	( )
7. Reliability, ability to complete assignments on time or to do what is asked of him	( )	( )	( )	( )
8. Achievement at levels beyond grade or group. Tendency to read ahead, do arithmetic examples other than asked, skill with science materials or experiments not shown in textbook, etc.	( )	( )	( )	( )
9. Ability to finish what he starts	( )	( )	( )	( )
10. Creativity, as revealed in degree of imagination shown in writing, music, art, science work	( )	( )	( )	( )
11. Creativity, ability to think out problems, readiness to take short cuts to achieve end	( )	( )	( )	( )
12. Conformity, tendency not to deviate from normal patterns of				

Nature of Skill or Characteristic	*low*	*average*	*high*	*superior*
work, play. Willingness to follow directions or regulations established by teacher or school	( )	( )	( )	( )
13. Alertness, ability to note details, something new or unusual	( )	( )	( )	( ).
14. Curiosity, wide range of interests, a desire to know how, why, and when things happened	( )	( )	( )	( )
15. Memory, ability to remember rules, regulations, details, facts or knowledge studied earlier	( )	( )	( )	( )
16. Discriminating skill, ability to sense what is important or significant	( )	( )	( )	( )
17. Speed in learning new things	( )	( )	( )	( )
18. Persistence, ability to continue working at a task in the face of obstacles or lack of equipment	( )	( )	( )	( )
19. Multiplicity of interests, has numerous hobbies, can always find something to occupy time	( )	( )	( )	( )
20. Skill in problem solving, ability to set up a new problem as well as solve those encountered in the course of a day	( )	( )	( )	( )
21. Vocabulary, ability to express himself through the use of descriptive words which he understands and uses correctly	( )	( )	( )	( )
22. Ability to accept a challenge, readiness to go beyond the minimum, ability to try and then complete a task which may appear difficult and even frustrating	( )	( )	( )	( )
23. Ability to work with abstract ideas. Needs a minimum of concrete experiences to grasp new ideas or concepts	( )	( )	( )	( )

Nature of Skill or Characteristic	*low*	*average*	*high*	*superior*
24. Generalization skill, ability to formulate a principle and proceed to test it out	( )	( )	( )	( )
25. Ability to take the initiative without being told	( )	( )	( )	( )
26. Ability to make critical judgments, to sense what is good, right, wrong, bad	( )	( )	( )	( )
27. Work shows skills have been mastered or information acquired which has meaning to the student	( )	( )	( )	( )
28. Ability to apply skill or use knowledge to solve problems, does not have to copy from the book	( )	( )	( )	( )
29. Quality of workmanship, pupil tends to hand in work which is of high quality, both in content and form	( )	( )	( )	( )
30. Reads widely, is not content to just sit when his work is done and library books or references are available	( )	( )	( )	( )
31. Leadership, inclination to serve in a leadership rather than follower position	( )	( )	( )	( )
32. Emotional development, seems to be able to accept new ideas, face challenges or change without becoming outwardly frustrated	( )	( )	( )	( )
33. Social acceptance, ability to get along with other boys and girls of his own age, or somewhat older	( )	( )	( )	( )
34. Readiness to volunteer, willingness to take on new assignments or take over duties not always desired by others	( )	( )	( )	( )
35. Attendance, regularity of attendance	( )	( )	( )	( )

Nature of Skill or Characteristic	low	average	high	superior
Composite or total rating divided by 35 (based on use of 1 for low, 2 for average, 3 for high and 4 for superior rating)				_____

Note: An average may be used as a guide point, but the differentiation of abilities may call for selective item analysis if one is trying to identify specific talents or skills.

The teacher may be asked to list the four or five students she considers superior in intellect or talent. She may then meet with the principal for a discussion of her recommendations. He may refer from time to time to cumulative record cards or anecdotal notes made by teachers who had worked previously with the pupils. Health records plus actual intelligence tests and achievement tests would supplement total scores or notations made on the cumulative record cards.

Home and family background and general behavior characteristics should be considered. If the two—teacher and principal—agree that a pupil is a potentially gifted student, the issue may be settled. If there is doubt in their minds, the assistance of others should be sought. On occasion the parents may be contacted for further information, but the usual procedure is to call for a meeting of several teachers who have worked closely with the student in question.

The school nurse and the physical education teacher are considered valuable persons to have on the new screening team because they generally see boys and girls in situations quite different from the normal classroom. The school psychologist will often bring out facts about the pupil's mental abilities or emotional patterns that are not always apparent to the teachers.

In a large school the coordinator of the program for gifted children may take the place of the principal or supervisor. He works with classroom teachers in an attempt to help them identify gifted and talented children.

He may provide outlines or check lists to help them refine their observations. He may visit regular as well as special classes to observe how pupils worked with and without close teacher direction. At other times he may seek out special subject teachers for their opinions, and if possible he will try to talk informally from time to time with pupils and parents. In the absence of the gifted child coordinator, guidance counselors often assist the principal and teacher in making recommendations for special classes or new programs for gifted or talented pupils.

Pupil Observations

Classroom teachers can learn a great deal about individual pupils in the classroom from observations that are made by their peermates. How boys and girls treat each other, how they work and play on the school grounds or at home and the interests they have outside the classroom will often help the teacher acquire a new insight into the potentialities of one or more students. One or more forms of sociometry can be used to obtain the benefit of pupil observations.

Very young children may respond to oral questions, but older pupils can respond easily to written questions. These may require simply a listing of pupils who have one or more of the characteristics given by the teacher, such as the following:

1. List three pupils with whom you would want to work if you were asked to write a play.

2. List three pupils whom you would want beside you if you had to walk late at night through (a) a dark forest, (b) a cemetery, or (c) a dangerous section of the city.

3. List three pupils whom you would like to have with you on a radio quiz program.

4. List three pupils with whom it would be most fun to spend the weekend on a lonely island.

5. List three pupils who would be good partners to have beside you as you ride the bus to visit _____.

The informal discussion will give teachers an insight into the kind of thinking that goes into the answers.

Parental Observations

Parents can often give new insight into the capabilities and interests of children. Frequently, parent conferences or even a home visit will help teachers understand the problems, interests or needs of children. Sometimes a questionnaire provides background information that is not found on cumulative record cards. In some schools a questionnaire is completed by parents prior to a visit to the school. It then becomes the basis for a special meeting with teacher, nurse, principal or school psychologist.

Observations of Community Leaders

Contacts with a boy scout leader, a minister, a playground director, a Little League sponsor and other community leaders will often prove helpful to those who are seeking information about potentially gifted children. What the children do outside of school can be important. For example, the teacher may want to know about their special skills in nonacademic areas or she may want to know how they react to pressures other than those exerted by the school. If boys and girls belong to a riding club, are members of a swimming team, take dancing or music lessons or attend Saturday morning arts and crafts classes, there should be someone who could tell the teacher about pupil behavior and work patterns that are not always apparent in the classroom. Individually and with the help of others the average teacher can discover characteristics of giftedness that will supplement the results of standardized testing programs.

3 *The Problem of Non-Recognition*

Each year thousands of boys and girls leave school without possession of the high school diploma so essential for success in a world that is crowding out the uninformed or poorly educated individual. These dropouts are failures in their own eyes as well as in those of their families and the society in which they live. Each boy and girl is a part of the nation's resources that is lost, but the tragedy is that many of these frustrated individuals possess high intelligence and talent. All too often the assumption is made that dropouts are just slow learners who have gone about as far as they can go in school and who, if they had stayed in school, would have held back the progress of those who wanted to learn. While there are many dropouts who leave school because they have reached the "learning plateau" for their intellects, a good number have reserves of energy, enthusiasm, interest, creative ideas and growth potential that could be released to the benefit of both society and themselves. Perhaps the greatest waste of the resources of our country lies in the teeming cities and empty rural areas where boys and girls go through school for a time without anyone recognizing the importance of their hidden abilities.

Yearly thousands of boys and girls graduate from high

school. For many of them the period of formal education is over. Some will marry almost immediately. Others will enter the work pool or a branch of the military. Friends, parents and relatives will give a sigh of relief because these young people have "made it." They are educated.

Unfortunately, this conclusion is not true for a large number of our graduates, especially those whose high intellect or special talents were never given the opportunity to develop. Does the average high school principal stop to think for a moment about each graduate clasping his hand and to ask: "Do I really know this boy? this girl?" It will be easy to recall something about the outstanding scholar, athlete or renegade non-conformist, but many of the graduates will have finished school leaving no imprint upon the school or the teachers who have worked with them. In this vast unknown student body there will be a large number of individuals who have the resource of giftedness. If this hidden strength has not been identified by those trained to educate, there is little hope that it will ever be discovered once the boy or girl becomes a part of the adult world.

In September of each year thousands of young men and women begin to study at an advanced level. It may be a junior college, a business school, a college or university. These students tend to be a select group. If they have one resource in common, it is that of an above-average intellect. They have passed through the weeding-out period and apparently have mastered those skills or the accumulated knowledge essential for admission to an institution of higher learning. Unfortunately, only a handful will ultimately graduate from college, and only a mere fraction of those who do will overcome the hurdle of graduate school. Many reasons for failure at these levels may be given, but the ultimate question is, "Would success at the college level have been possible if elementary and secondary schools had done things differently?" Perhaps society is expecting too much of the millions who begin college but fail to complete it. Yet for many the answer still lies in the failure of our schools to set the stage for adult living. This is especially true of those of our elementary and secondary school students who coast and drift through school.

The Need for Teachers to Recognize Giftedness

The search for gifted children is often difficult if teachers do not understand what it is they are looking for. There are many clues to work with, but teachers often fail to find them. As a result numerous talented and gifted children are overlooked by those who would identify them and establish special programs for their maximum development. Studies have shown that the average teacher needs help in detecting gifted children and then in planning special activities for them based on their specialized abilities or talents. When asked to select gifted children for extra attention, teachers have repeatedly pointed out pupils with average ability who could never compete with truly gifted children despite their good work habits. On other occasions they have just failed to recognize any pupils with high potentialities. One study of the results of group intelligence tests administered to over 1500 elementary and junior high school pupils indicated the need to do something constructive for all of the children designated as possessing high intelligence. While approximately 60 per cent of the pupils had IQ's over 115, the 100 teachers who were asked to identify those pupils who could be considered especially talented or gifted listed only five pupils. The administrators may have been at fault in not defining the term *gifted* with and for the teachers. Many potentially gifted pupils with IQ's in the 120 to 135 category could have been overlooked because teachers were thinking in limited instead of broad terms.

Individual teachers who work closely with gifted children should, on the basis of common sense alone, be able to spot potentially gifted children. However, this is not always the case. A first grade pupil had no difficulty with number work ordinarily not introduced until fourth grade; yet the classroom teacher saw no need to take the girl out of the first grade arithmetic readiness program which was of no value to her. A second grade pupil, reading encyclopedias and technical science books and pamphlets, showed the ability to concentrate his attention for large blocks of time on materials far beyond the comprehension of average fifth and sixth grade pupils; yet he was not considered above normal intelligence in the eyes of the classroom teacher.

Prior to the division of a new first grade class into reading subgroups, teachers in many school systems over-look the significance of the ability to read with speed and comprehension. This ability to master the skills of formal reading at an early age is one of the character-istics of gifted children. It should be a warning to the teacher that normal teaching activities will not suffice if these children are to be properly motivated and encour-aged to proceed from their advanced starting position. This is where nongraded classes or balanced grouping will help the teacher plan more effectively for such chil-dren. In some instances pupils may not have acquired proficiency in an area by the time they reach first grade; but within a short time potentially gifted pupils will begin to achieve success in reading and writing so fast that they do not fit into any normal first grade class. In one school two first grade teachers used the buddy system to restruc-ture their classes in order to form one fast-moving teach-able group from the two classrooms. In a larger school system such pupils could readily be sent to a special class for gifted pupils, but here again the need for special attention must first be recognized.

It is easy enough for teachers to administer all the tests described in the previous chapter; the problem lies in interpreting the data and then doing something positive about the learning situation. It is not enough to know that three fifth grade students have IQ's above 130 or that a cumulative record card shows potential high levels of intelligence. The big problem is that of making teachers understand what these scores mean in terms of the role *they* must play in the educational process.

The average teacher works with average children. Her curriculum is built for average children. The books assigned to her are based on programs of study for average children and the school year is adapted to achievement levels to be reached by average boys and girls in approximately 180 days. The teacher knows that she is going to have a problem with a number of slow learners; therefore, at least at the elementary school level, she will make special efforts to bring them up to grade level. Unfortunately, these same teachers will not do as much for the gifted children. In many cases the mistake is one of not understanding the teacher's role in the education of gifted children. The teacher is prone to think, "I can't do any more. I'm exhausted when I go home now, so how can I be expected to provide for the gifted?" Intellectually gifted and talented boys and girls need teachers to guide them and help them, but their needs can be met without imposing impossible demands upon the teachers. In many classrooms—if some traditional barriers of the school could be changed—their special talents could become assets to the teacher who feels overworked. For example, many gifted pupils would gladly assume leadership roles in the classroom if the teacher would create a setting that would give them opportunities to assume responsibilities. The conflict arises when the teacher tries to assume a dominant role in all learning activities.

Teachers and principals who accept responsibility for a full program of educational activities for all children cannot ignore the needs of the upper quarter of their student body. If they understand the true meaning of giftedness, they must break with traditions. Grouping practices within a school or classroom need to be changed, and the concept of the grade with its learning-time limits needs to be modified. Perhaps the answer to the problem of educating gifted children lies in the development of school and classroom flexibility guided by technology. Here is where mechanized instruments such as the computer can assist in the scheduling of pupils and classes on the basis of need. For example, cross-grade grouping or nongraded classes can be formed on the basis of common needs, interests or achievements by the use of regional computers. This would eliminate much of the duplication found in most classes in arithmetic, reading, spelling and so on. Bright pupils who have reached the stage of advanced learning would not have to be subjected to a shotgun approach to learning. Trial-and-error teaching could be replaced by direct teaching on the basis of recognition of strengths and weaknesses.

Perhaps the error of our schools lies in the interpretation of the word *gifted*. Few educators gave anything more than lip service to the needs of gifted and talented children until the mid-1950's. During this decade numerous articles were written, research and special programs for gifted children were instituted in a number of school systems for the first time. It has taken time for the entire teaching staff of most school systems to become aware of the responsibility each one shares in the education of such children. For a time the word *gifted* was used with a bit of awe, as a term referring to the so-called genius and to those pupils classified by Terman as having superior intelligence. Since this included less than 2 per cent of the total population, the teacher's direct contact with gifted children was relatively limited. However, the tendency to consider pupils with lower IQ's has increased teacher contacts with gifted children to the point where they can no longer ignore their responsibilities. If the term is broadened even further to include the potentially talented as well as the intellectually endowed, the seriousness of the problem is more acute than ever, because special consideration becomes mandatory for a potential 30 per cent of the children in an average community and an even higher percentage in a school drawing from a very high socioeconomic segment of the school district.

Reasons for Non-Identification of the Gifted

Many reasons can be given for the failure of teachers to identify potentially gifted children in their classrooms. At times teachers will admit to their failures, but the reasons given will not always be the real ones because conscientious teachers may not understand why they overlook attributes frequently associated with talented or intellectually gifted boys and girls. For example, potentially talented boys may not be listed as candidates for special consideration because they are nonconformists. As a result, such students may have to work exceptionally hard to achieve recognition from their teachers. This is often evident when teachers are grading papers—that is, the pupil who conforms to the teacher's personal standards will receive his rewards much faster and more easily than the pupil who deviates markedly from them.

Gifted pupils may not be recognized because of the following:

1. *Teachers continue to think in terms of stereotypes.* Many gifted pupils have good working relationships with their peermates. They do not exhibit characteristics frequently associated with the stereotypes commonly portrayed in movies, cartoons or stories; therefore, the stamp of *gifted* is never placed upon them. They are too normal for their own good.

2. *Cumulative records have not been adequately kept.* During a pupil's school career numerous tests for intelligence or achievement are given that could point up the possibility that characteristics of giftedness are present. Unfortunately, much of these data are lost or placed on cumulative records, so they have little meaning to those who turn to them for guidance or direction. For example, several IQ's will be listed on a card without reference to the type of test they were based on. In one school the results of costly Stanford-Binet intelligence tests were mixed with group intelligence test scores. It was impossible for the teacher to tell which of several scores was

most representative of the true mental capacity of selected students. For example, Mildred had reported IQ's of 118, 132 and 145. The cumulative record card was of little help to the teacher because she could not tell which test had been used to classify the pupil. In this case the school psychologist was available and could produce the original test that he had administered, showing a Stanford-Binet rating of 145. Subsequent testing showed that this was apparently Mildred's true potential.

More often, in many schools test data are reported in terms of average achievement or average intelligence. It may be easier to record data this way, but many of the subsections of standardized tests can point up special strengths of the potentially gifted. For example, the high verbal intelligence score may be obscured in averaging by the low nonverbal score. Also, reading may be recorded as an average, thus concealing a weakness in reading comprehension skill. Similarly, a composite achievement score eliminates any reference to a strength in arithmetic, spelling, language or other areas where pupils may have demonstrated proficiency. If school records are to be kept accurately, responsibility for the entry of all significant data should be bestowed upon clerks who are trained to record dates, names of tests and the types of information considered essential by the professional educator. Teachers can be excellent in the classroom but absolute failures in record-keeping. As a rule they do not enjoy this responsibility; also, they frequently have to complete cumulative records at a busy time of year, as a result of which errors may occur more easily. If several teachers work with a set of record cards over a period of years, it becomes impossible to detect errors and omissions or to assign responsibility for them to one person; therefore, all permanent record cards should be kept up to date by nonprofessional members of the teaching staff but under the direction of those who know what should be included in a complete cumulative record.

3. *Teachers have not been able to abstract or interpret data included on permanent records.* Many teachers can

look at a record card without learning anything from the mass of words and figures. This may be due to their lack of experience or failure to understand the significance of test scores, pupil grades or previous teacher comments. Often, teachers have never had any introduction to the principles of tests and measurements, so words like *percentile, grade equivalent* or *validity* may have little meaning for them. The fact that test scores or grades taken from different tests or teachers have little relationship to each other may completely escape them. A trained observer may see clues in the fact that pupil achievement on the part of an eighth grader has consistently matched expected achievement for one or more mental ability tests administered at earlier grade levels. The existence of high achievement and high intelligence scores in the face of repeated negativistic teacher comments or low report card grades may indicate a need for immediate study of the pupil's work-study relationships in the classroom. In some instances a difference in teacher philosophy will be reflected in the comments teachers make about pupils or in the marks they assign to pupils. This was apparent in a school where one out of four teachers recorded achievement and accomplishments in terms of *ability* instead of the traditional grade standards. This made comparisons of different teacher reports impossible since the basis for the ability marks was not evident.

4. *Teachers do not see the values of standardized tests.* Many school teachers will administer standardized tests and yet will not see the value in them. All too often the tests are given and scored and the test results recorded without anything constructive being done as a result of the testing program. The extreme futility of a testing program was found in a training school supposedly working on behalf of bright pupils; in this school the principal kept test scores locked up in a safe where teachers could not have access to them. In a good educational system the standardized tests are used constructively to improve instruction, to help in the identification of gifted children and to attend to the special needs of all children.

In some other schools teachers are suspicious of standardized test results. A common complaint is that boys and girls guess, and therefore, the test scores are not valid. Although some pupils may guess too freely, the teachers should remember that the standardized test is only one measure in the total evaluative process. Properly administered and used in conjunction with teacher judgment and other evidence, these tests become a valuable aid to the teacher.

5. *Too much emphasis is placed on a single test score.* Children have been improperly labeled on the basis of a single test score. This has led to frustration on the part of the gifted pupil whose talent was not recognized as well as to frustrations on the part of average learners who, because of high motivation, good home backgrounds and other factors, were placed in learning situations that laid stress on achieving at levels beyond their true potential. No single achievement or intelligence test should be used to classify children or to assign them to advanced programs.

6. *Too much emphasis has been placed upon teacher marks.* Since teacher marks tend to be highly subjective, there is danger in placing too much emphasis upon them. Teacher marks may not reflect a pupil's true achievement level or potential. The day-by-day program may not provide a challenge to pupils, so they make little effort to exert themselves. In many cases grades made by boys or by pupils from deprived cultural areas will not be as high as those of girls or of pupils coming from better home environments.

7. *Too much emphasis has been placed on grade norms.* Teachers have accepted achievement at the class norm or slightly above it as satisfactory. In doing so, they have failed to consider the actual potential of the student and at what level he should be achieving if his accomplishments were based upon actual mental ability and not that of a class or grade in a particular school.

8. *Poor readers have been designated as slow learners.* Gifted individuals who for one reason or another fail to

master high-level reading skills have been placed in the same category as slow learners. All too often parents and teachers fail to realize that inability to read is the result of many factors, some of which may be beyond the control of the individual. For example, exposure to faulty reading techniques at an early age or the absence of challenging reading materials can turn intellectually gifted children away from reading. This inability to read will often be reflected in the pupil's low achievement in subjects having a reading base.

9. *Teachers have failed to look for giftedness among disadvantaged children.* Teachers tend to look for gifted children among those who come from more favored homes. Although a much higher number of gifted children can be identified on the basis of family background and cultural background, teachers should not make the assumption that bright children will not be found coming from poor homes or from families where one or both parents have little if any education.

10. *Teacher prejudice may deter the recognition of talent.* The mores of a segment of the community that does not conform to those of the teacher may affect the teacher's attitude toward those pupils who possess what may be described as low social class standards. Pupils who do not dress, talk, write or act in terms of the teacher's standards may not be recognized as having qualities associated with giftedness. This will make pupils from low socioeconomic areas reject school and the goals established for their protection and well-being. Potentially gifted pupils will have some hidden talents regardless of their home backgrounds; however, they need understanding and encouragement in a school environment where teachers understand that creative actions or accomplishments can stem from those who have broken with tradition or the accepted way of doing things at home.

11. *Gifted pupils who are disciplinary problems may not be recognized.* Boys and girls who repeatedly break teacher rules or school rules are not popular with teachers or principals. Their nonconformist actions tend to help

stigmatize them. For example, if they show high achievement in one or more areas of the curriculum, their accomplishments may be overlooked. This may not be with any malicious intent, but give a boy a bad name and it takes a great deal of effort to erase the suspicion that he will not revert to his old ways. There is, for example, always the feeling that the pupil who was caught cheating will continue to do so—but more furtively. Unfortunately, high accomplishment by such individuals may be questioned even when it is the result of honest effort and work.

12. *Teachers fail to recognize emotionally disturbed children.* Highly gifted children who have extreme emotional problems may not be recognized. In many cases this is due to a lack of teacher awareness of her role in the learning situation. Most teachers are not prepared to work with emotionally disturbed boys and girls, especially those who need to work in a more controlled environment than the standard classroom with large-sized classes.

13. *Socially immature pupils may not be recognized.* The extremely shy or highly introverted pupils may fail to let the teacher know what they can do or how they think. A less talented extrovert who is not always correct in his statements may rate higher in the teacher's estimate than the gifted pupil who lacks the self-confidence necessary to stand up and give correct answers.

14. *A lack of enthusiasm for learning can be serious.* Gifted pupils are supposed to enjoy schooling. They are supposed to be enthusiastic about science, mathematics and learning in general. When they fail to demonstrate this enthusiasm, the teacher is likely to overlook their more outstanding characteristics. In doing so, the teachers may merely perpetuate learning situations that have *destroyed* the challenge that may have existed when the boy or girl first entered kindergarten.

15. *Pupil mobility can prevent the recognition of talent.* Many parents are on the move constantly; therefore, pupils may not remain in a school long enough to demonstrate what they can do. Pupil records are lost or

may just never be forwarded. The teacher and principal may never get together the evidence needed for proper identification of talented boys and girls who attend many schools during their journeys across the country or city. (This is one reason why central clearing houses for pupil records would help in the proper placement of children who are new to a school.)

16. *Teachers do not know many children as boys and girls.* Teachers who see children only in the formal classroom setting may not know them as real live boys and girls. Some children conceal their fears, their dreams and their interests from the teacher. As a result the teacher may never understand what they are trying to do or say. Unless the curriculum is broad and the teacher promotes activities that will help draw children out or place them in different learning situations, giftedness may not be seen. Artistically-, musically-, scientifically- or mechanically-inclined children need opportunities to apply their skills. In many instances they have hobbies and interests that never enter the world of the classroom.

17. *Teachers need help in establishing a criterion for making judgments.* The average classroom teacher will be more effective in her judgments if she has the assistance of other teachers, a principal, supervisor, school psychologists or other specialists. Sometimes a workshop will help bring out characteristics of gifted children that would otherwise be overlooked. Here a team approach will help in the evaluative process; collectively, the teachers who have had an opportunity to study the characteristics of giftedness or talent will be able to refine their procedures. They may use a number of criteria that will lead to early identification of gifted or talented boys and girls.

Identifying Underachievers

Concern over pupil dropout and failure at high school and college levels has led to studies of underachievers with superior ability. These studies show that 15 to 25 per cent with IQ's of 120 or better may be classified as underachievers on the basis of (1) failure to obtain satisfactory grades and (2) failure to make high scores on standardized achievement tests. Many of the pupils falling into the first category scored higher on standardized achievement tests than teachers gave them credit for in terms of class accomplishment. In the latter category were numerous pupils who failed to demonstrate achievement on the tests commensurate with their report card grades. In some communities it is found that the number of underachievers with superior ability exceeds 25 per cent. The problem is complicated by the fact that twice as many boys as girls fall into the underachievement category.

Remedial instruction is often recommended for underachievers, but tutoring or special instruction in reading or study skills does not reverse patterns that have become fixed over a long period of time. As a result of clinical and psychological studies such as the New York City Talent Preservation Project educators have come to the conclusion that work patterns that lead to underachievement have their start in elementary and junior high school grades. About half the boys with superior intellect are considered underachievers by the time they reach grade 11 or grade 12, but some of them show a tendency towards underachievement as early as the first grade. In most schools there is a small number of underachievers in grades 2 and 3, with a steady increase becoming noticeable as one goes from grades 3 through 11. Surprisingly, girls tend to show up as above average in scholastic studies until they reach grade 5. From grade 6 through grade 11 the girls show a sharp decrease in academic interests and achievement. The elementary teachers are urged to do all they can to identify underachievers as early as possible and then strive to carry out a program that will keep them working at levels commensurate with their ability.

The teacher's role is made difficult because the causes of underachievement vary from one individual to another. A number of factors are in force at one time, some having their origin in the school, others lying in the home or community. Early identification of giftedness is essential because kindergarten and first grade teachers can observe characteristics associated with giftedness that are covered up as boys and girls get older. Moreover, the teacher can plan a more effective program for gifted children if she knows the nature of the material she has to work with at the start. If children need or are capable of benefiting from a special program, the earlier it is started the better. Because of differences in cultural backgrounds it may not be possible to identify some gifted pupils or underachievers until they reach the intermediate grades. This makes it imperative for the school to develop and maintain records that will help teachers and other specialists in the continued identification of underachievement throughout the child's school years. Teachers must be prepared to use anecdotal records, clinical reports, readiness tests, intelligence test records, achievement test scores, aptitude tests, health records, reports of actual pupil progress in reading and other subjects and an examination of pupil work-study patterns to supplement their own observations.

Many people do not realize how valuable guidance can be for many elementary school children. Even though teachers may give them help, there are some pupils who would benefit if more elementary schools had one or more trained guidance counselors who could help both teachers and pupils who have problems of growth and adjustment. These individuals must work closely with pupils of all abilities, but special consideration is recommended for students at the 75th percentile of the ability scale as well as those at the 25th percentile level. While they work with boys and girls they must continually review school marks, reading achievement or accomplishment, test scores and teacher estimates regarding pupil ability and achievement.

The Unrecognized Problems of Gifted Children

Underachievement can be serious to every boy or girl but to a boy or girl who has the mentality associated with giftedness it can be a real tragedy. How far he goes in life may depend upon his ability to use talents that few people are fortunate enough to possess. Yet many boys and girls fail to realize what it means to waste their potential power. To be popular and accepted by their peermates, some of them may conceal their ability to complete assignments quickly and with enjoyment. A pupil who has talent in art and music may find ready acceptance by some of his peermates whereas his parents may condemn his efforts as being time-consuming and wasteful. He should be out working or studying, they feel, if he is going to amount to anything.

Social acceptance and recognition can be a problem for the young adolescent and teen-ager. Girls, for example, may try to conceal their real interests and skills from boy friends who cannot compete with them in an intellectual field. The adolescent boy may find his interest in music is in conflict with his desire to play ball and be with the gang; he has only a few spare hours in the day, so a choice must be made between essential practice on a musical instrument and practice on the ball field. For many youngsters high school brings about an end to those long years of music instruction. Homework and outside interests take precedence over older interests.

Probably the greatest problem gifted children face is one of guidance. Many of them want help but do not know where to turn to obtain it. The fact that many of these children have multiple interests can be an asset but the decision to pursue a specific interest can be a difficult one. Talent may be overlooked because of an apparent interest that allows the student to obtain an immediate reward, which he prefers to years of study or work and a deferred reward. Sometimes a multiplicity of choices leads to continued confusion and frustration. At the opposite pole is the individual whose talent or special interest is submerged by forces beyond his control, leaving him devoid of a goal and lacking in motivation. All his life he may wonder what might have been had some teacher, friend or parent intervened to help him over a barrier that he could not climb alone.

One of the burdens that talented people may have to face is the fact that they seldom have anyone to understand them. For example, the genius who elects to remain on a college campus may find a comradeship and understanding that he may never find in a small community where intellectualism is not appreciated. The great mathematician, scientist, poet, musician or architect may be respected, but each one can make ordinary people feel uncomfortable. While this is more likely to be true at the adult level, there are some teachers in the lower grades who feel insecure teaching a class where extremely bright and talented students anticipate what teachers say and do and where they may know more than the instructor. In such classes the promising student may find himself rebuffed and rejected at a very time when sympathy, encouragement and recognition are most sorely needed.

Underlying Causes of Problems of Gifted Children

Upper grade pupils may have to make greater adjustments than primary grade pupils because they are more sensitive to external pressures. At both age levels teachers will find pupils making adjustments as a result of factors they cannot control. Those pupils who learn to adjust their work and play patterns may find life continues to have a constant challenge and thrill, but failure to secure the answers they seek can lead to resistance and an attempt to fight back at the world in retaliation as they try to cope with problems originating from some of the following:

1. A desire to be accepted by their peers in school and nonschool activities.

2. Their classmates' resentment of the ease with which they work and solve academic problems and the approval they receive from teachers and other adults because of their superior accomplishments.

3. A tendency on the part of teachers to recognize and reward academic achievement in terms of results rather than processes and/or creativity.

4. The failure of teachers to recognize the value of skill in manipulative activities and of social and physical development of gifted pupils.

5. The failure of teachers to recognize the inherent values to be found in the fine arts—music, art, dramatics, creative writing, the dance—and in other areas of the curriculum that are less academic in nature than reading, writing and arithmetic.

6. The failure of the school to provide enough challenging experiences. All too often gifted children are not free to use the overabundance of free time, which they cannot manage without help.

7. The tendency of parents, friends and siblings to minimize their accomplishments and dreams.

8. A failure to develop sound work habits or to develop the ability to maintain sustained effort. This may be due to the fact that they have seldom had to exert themselves to complete assignments, but it could be due to an inadequate introduction to fundamental processes and work-study patterns at lower grade levels.

9. A dislike for essential drill and repetition because it interferes with other, more satisfying interests.

10. A feeling of frustration because

    a) goals have been set that are still beyond their advanced stage of development.

    b) they still lack the breadth of experience essential for the mastery or understanding of abstractions.

    c) they fail to see how they can use special abilities or talents to meet obligations to home, school and society.

11. A desire to become perfect before essential skills or

talents are developed. Handwriting skill, control of a paintbrush and so forth may have to be deferred until muscular coordination is perfected.

12. The frustrations of and even jealousies of teachers who cannot compete with pupils who have developed a superior skill or more understanding than the teachers have. Some of these teachers deliberately or unintentionally discourage them with ridicule, sarcasm or by ignoring them.

13. A resistance to school and teachers because of repeated exposure to meaningless recitations, lectures and busy-work assignments that gave them no feeling of accomplishment.

14. Their curiosity or their overexuberance, which has sometimes made them so aggressive that other pupils ridicule them or torment them because they always have the answer first and never seem to make a mistake.

15. Their tendency to overlook their own limitations or to be overobsessed with their own importance or capacity. They may be unable to evaluate the results of their efforts correctly so that they will become truly self-directive or self-appraising.

16. Their lack of patience with slower-learning pupils who have spent long and painful hours in achieving what they, the gifted pupils, have mastered in a short span of time.

17. Their development of a strong dislike for their own powers because these talents set them apart from their peermates.

18. Their gaining either too much or too little recognition for their efforts.

19. Their sometimes failing to develop essential skills that will give them a balance. A one-sided development may earn them the title of being just another "character."

20. Their occasionally expending such an excessive amount of time and effort pursuing hobbies that they neglect to fulfill obligations to others as well as to themselves.

21. The economic, social and physical pressures that

may force them to pursue lines of endeavor other than those wherein their special interests and talents lie.

22. Leadership qualities never being recognized because these pupils are never placed in situations where they can demonstrate their ability to assume responsibility and guide or direct others.

23. The lack of access to resource materials in school or at home that would lead to the stimulation of interests or a challenge to explore further into selected fields of study—that is, supplementary readers, current magazines, pamphlets, up-to-date encyclopedias, records, films, film strips and library books.

24. Failure to achieve close to desired accomplishment levels may be attributed to the influence of a broken home. Studies show more fatherless families exist among low achievers than among high achievers.

25. Low achievement may originate in physical factors ranging from a problem of laterality or handedness to an extreme physical defect. In some cases a lack of physical strength has lowered a bright pupil's enduring powers. The individual may have had high educational goals but required more sleep and rest than comparable peermates who could devote endless hours to the mastery of an assignment or project.

26. The lack of flexibility in the curriculum, the insistence on rigid grade standards and the continuation of a practice of holding talented boys and girls back to prevent any encroachment upon the next teacher's domain. This may be responsible for low achievement in areas of the curriculum other than reading, as a result of the limited growth or stretching of the mind in areas like arithmetic, science or social studies unless there is an opportunity to move into newer and higher concepts under the direction of a teacher.

27. The lack of sufficient imagination on the part of teachers to cope with gifted children's needs and interests and frequent teacher failure to recognize the "lazy," "indifferent," "daydreamer," or "behavior-problem" child as an *anxious child*.

28. Failure of parents and teachers to insist on quality work or high standards. This is especially true of underachievers in need of remedial assistance.

29. Individuals may fail to achieve at desired levels because of emotional instability. This imbalance in emotional control may range from a moderate childish impulsiveness to an extreme where the individual finds it difficult to work in a class situation.

30. Intellectual curiosity is often considered as an outstanding trait of gifted children. Unfortunately, there are gifted underachievers who are totally lacking in curiosity. This is reflected in their low accomplishment even in special classes for the gifted where their learning environment is conducive to the fullest development of their talents or intellectual potential.

One area of concern which has been neglected until recently is that of the gifted underachiever's self-concept. Studies by the Horace Mann Institute, the Portland Public Schools, the Evanston Township High School, and the De Witt Clinton High School in New York City lend emphasis to the need to help underachievers acquire a better self-concept. Unfortunately, it may be too late to start such a program at the high school level since negativistic attitudes for these youngsters may be fairly well fixed even by the time they reach junior high school. Studies by Brookover, Payne and Farquhar, and Fink show that a positive relationship exists between the individual's self-concept in a given subject and his accomplishments in that subject. Thus, high achievers tend to do well in areas where they have a high self-concept, and low achievers tend to achieve at low levels in areas where their self-concept is low.

Due to the rationalization that often occurs when guidance counselors work with low achieving students, it is not always easy to locate the real reason for an individual's poor showing. For example, a bright student may cast the blame for his low performance rating on adults who are always picking on him when in reality his problem dates back to the fact that he has been frustrated by a school curriculum that measured achievement constantly in terms of language factors instead of the non-language factors which characterize his strength. Again, the individual's hostility to school activities may reflect an exposure to a cultural environment that does not support high educational goals. To admit that parents, siblings and peermates think very little of the educational goals promoted by well-meaning teachers would be to betray his home and friends. This barrier may never appear on the surface, but it can make itself felt by aggressive actions against classmates and teachers at the primary grade level. Thus, hostility and rejection of the school may reflect a confusion due to the conflict of two opposing cultural worlds.

The Problem of Recognition in Different Communities

The problem of providing for gifted children in the classroom depends upon the nature of the community because the number of such pupils in a school varies in proportion to the socioeconomic level of the children's background. In an average community children with an IQ of 115 will often stand out academically, but in a high socioeconomic community the number of children with intelligence quotients above 115 may be so great that the mere 115 IQ pupil will be overshadowed constantly by a preponderance of more capable peermates. He may be considered the equivalent of an average learner instead of a superior one. The problems involved in establishing a program for gifted children are very different in these communities because the proportion of gifted children to nongifted children may be three times as great in a wealthy suburban community as it is in the average small city or small town. Tables 4 and 5 will give the reader a picture of the various needs of different types of communities.

Table 4 shows the approximate number of gifted children that may be anticipated in schools housing 600

Table 4. POTENTIAL NUMBER OF GIFTED AND NONGIFTED PUPILS IN SCHOOLS LOCATED IN COMMUNITIES CLASSIFIED AS AVERAGE AND ABOVE AVERAGE SOCIALLY AND ECONOMICALLY

Approximate per cent and number of pupils possessing IQ's in designated intellectual ranges that may be found in two 600-pupil schools located in communities with distinctly different socioeconomic levels.

	No. of gifted pupils in an average community			No. of gifted pupils in high socioeconomic level community	
Stanford-Binet IQ range	Per cent	No. of Pupils	Stanford-Binet IQ range	Per cent	No. of pupils
140 and above	1.0	6	140 and above	3.0	18
135 to 139	1.0	6	135 to 139	4.0	24
130 to 134	2.1	13	130 to 134	5.3	32
125 to 129	3.1	19	125 to 129	9.3	56
120 to 124	5.1	31	120 to 124	12.4	74
115 to 119	8.1	49	115 to 119	15.0	90
Total gifted	20.4	124		49.0	294

No. of gifted pupils in an average community

Stanford-Binet IQ range	Per cent	No. of Pupils
110 to 114	10.0	60
105 to 109	10.6	64
100 to 104	12.9	77
95 to 99	14.2	85
90 to 94	9.1	55
85 to 89	8.8	53
80 to 84	5.7	34
Under 80	8.3	48
Total nongifted	79.6	428
Total	100.0	600

No. of gifted pupils in high socioeconomic level community

Stanford-Binet IQ range	Per cent	No. of pupils
110 to 114	15.0	90
105 to 109	12.0	72
100 to 104	10.0	60
95 to 99	7.0	42
90 to 94	3.5	21
85 to 89	2.1	13
80 to 84	.9	5
Under 80	.5	3
Total nongifted	51.0	306
Total	100.0	600

pupils but located in what may be classified as average and high socioeconomic level communities. The figures are only potential since they are based on the assumption that the average community will have the same spread of intelligence as that found in the Stanford-Binet Intelligence Scale. The potential number of gifted children found in the high socioeconomic level community is based on an estimated tripling of the number found at the upper levels of giftedness, with a gradual reduction in the percentages in terms of the curve established on a probability scale.

Table 5 gives the picture of the spread of intelligence in five separate New York State communities. Three of these communities are actual high socioeconomic communities from three distinct parts of the state. Community number four represents an average community for all of New York State, but it is actually superior in terms of the anticipated level of the nation.* Community number five is classified as a below-average community for the state, but it would be closer to the norm for the United States. The figures in this table show the existence of a very large number of apparently gifted children in the first three communities, which means that the curriculum of these schools should reflect an all-school emphasis on the needs of talented and gifted pupils. Since the number of potentially talented children in the fifth school system is relatively small, teachers are quite apt to minimize the need for a gifted pupil program.

If classification of gifted pupils is done on the basis of intelligence, the size and type of community will be factors that cannot be ignored. The elementary school with 600 pupils coming from an average socioeconomic level may have 5 or 6 potentially gifted children with IQ's of 140 or better. Since these children may be located anywhere from kindergarten to the sixth grade it will be

---

* Nationwide samplings of intelligence provide a mean IQ of 100 while a statewide testing program for New York State provides a mean of 108.5.

difficult to develop a full program for them. A similar-sized school located in a superior socioeconomic level community may have 18 potentially gifted children. This is still a small number of pupils to plan for because of the vast range in chronological ages. However, the picture changes rapidly with the adoption of a cutoff point of 130. Now the former community would have approximately 18 to 24 gifted pupils to educate whereas the more favored community would have from 73 to 83 gifted pupils to educate. This number would make it possible to establish special classes, either on a grade or mixed-grade basis.

Each time the cutoff point is lowered, the number of intellectually gifted pupils increases until there is a potential 20 per cent in need of special attention in the average community compared with a potential 60 per cent in the wealthy community.

At the other extreme is the community with a preponderance of disadvantaged children. A school drawing heavily from low socioeconomic levels will have few, if any, children who may be classified as intellectually gifted. In such a school the gifted individual may become a source of frustration to teacher and principal because it is impossible to assign him to a learning situation where his capabilities can be recognized among peermates of a comparable chronological age. Due to the lack of numbers, it is impossible to form a special class for gifted pupils that would provide the challenge needed for continuous growth. In one school of 1200 pupils the highest reported IQ was in the low 90's. While cultural factors may have limited the identification of potentially gifted children, the fact remains that any truly gifted individuals in such schools create teaching problems for the instructor. The only solution that seems practical in such schools is to identify the highest achievers or potentially gifted pupils and then to assign the students to a centrally located school with special classes.

Gifted children in rural areas or slum areas of a city will often be at a disadvantage because teachers cannot

Table 5 COMPARATIVE DISTRIBUTION OF POTENTIALLY GIFTED CHILDREN IN DIFFERENT NEW YORK STATE COMMUNITIES

Per cent of gifted and nongifted children in average and high socioeconomic level communities

IQ range	High socioeconomic community #1 Per cent	High socioeconomic community #2 Per cent	High socioeconomic community #3 Per cent	Average socioeconomic community in New York State Per cent	Below-average level community in New York State Per cent
150 to 154		.4			
145 to 149	.9	1.1	1.8	.8	
140 to 144	2.6	4.2	2.3	1.6	
135 to 139	5.2	10.9	7.0	2.3	
130 to 134	16.6	12.3	13.5	6.3	1.6
125 to 129	10.5	14.4	16.3	12.7	1.6
120 to 124	14.0	15.5	17.5	16.7	1.6
115 to 119	19.3	13.0	13.5	10.3	6.7
Total gifted	69.1	71.8	71.9	50.7	11.5

IQ range	High socioeconomic community #1 Per cent	High socioeconomic community #2 Per cent	High socioeconomic community #3 Per cent	Average socioeconomic community in New York State Per cent	Below-average level community in New York State Per cent
110 to 114	9.7	11.6	14.6	15.9	16.5
105 to 109	9.7	6.6	5.8	8.7	18.2
100 to 104	8.8	3.2	1.8	10.3	16.5
95 to 99	1.8	1.4	.6	3.2	10.0
90 to 94	.9	3.2	2.9	4.8	10.7
85 to 89			1.2	3.2	6.7
80 to 84		1.1	.6	2.4	5.0
75 to 79			.6	.8	
70 to 74		.7			.8
65 to 69					2.5
60 to 64					1.6
55 to 59		.4			
50 to 54					
Total nongifted	30.9	28.2	28.1	49.3	88.5
Total	100.0	100.0	100.0	100.0	100.0
Mean IQ	119.5	120.7	120.8	108.9	101.4

provide them with a program of activities or the work materials they need. While the problems of rural areas and slums may appear to be the same, geographic lines constitute more difficult problems for the educators who want to provide a more adequate program for the isolated farm or mountain boy. In contrast, the principal of an urban school may have access to professional workers and facilities that can help enrich the life of the culturally disadvantaged but talented student in a school where he is considered an isolate. Unfortunately, financial and political barriers will frequently pose problems to the urban principal who wants to institute a special program for potentially gifted children.

Table 6 presents a comparison of the distribution of intelligence in a New Jersey school system which falls into the high socioeconomic category with that of a neighboring community that approximates the norm for the nation. It should be apparent that the curriculum of the former community will have to be much different from the one in the latter community. For example, the average community with a mean IQ of 100 will have far fewer gifted children to provide for than the high socioeconomic community. This is evident in the fact that a cutoff point of 130 will leave only 5 per cent of the children in an average community in need of special attention whereas 26 per cent of the children in the wealthier community may be classified as deserving the type of education desired for intellectually gifted students. Similarly, a lowering of the cutoff point to 115 and above would increase the number of potentially gifted children in the average community to 18 per cent and to approximately 63 per cent in the community falling into the high socioeconomic category. If one were to superimpose on Table 6 the distribution of gifted children from a community classified as falling into the low socioeconomic category, the curve would show approximately .2 per cent falling into the 130 or better intelligence classification or approximately 2 per cent falling into the superior category, 115 IQ or better.

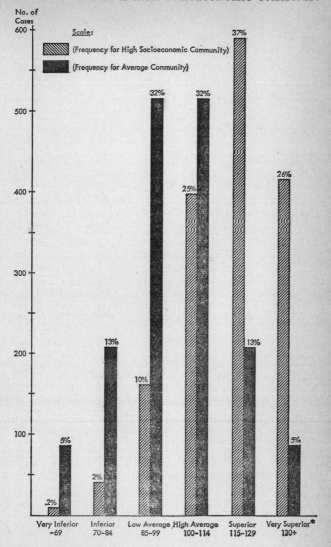

Table 6 A COMPARISON OF THE DISTRIBUTION OF
INTELLIGENCE IN AN AVERAGE COMMUNITY
AND IN A HIGH SOCIOECONOMIC COMMUNITY

No. of
Cases

Scale:
(Frequency for High Socioeconomic Community)
(Frequency for Average Community)

	Very Inferior -69	Inferior 70-84	Low Average 85-99	High Average 100-114	Superior 115-129	Very Superior* 130+
High Socioeconomic	.2%	2%	10%	25%	37%	26%
Average	5%	13%	32%	32%	13%	5%

*Based on California Test Bureau Classifications.

part two | *Meeting the Educational Needs of Gifted Children*

4 Meeting Needs Through Special Classes

There are varied approaches to the problems of our gifted pupils in our schools. In some communities external and internal pressures have led to the formation of special classes for gifted boys and girls. Special classes have been found mainly in cities such as New York, Birmingham (Alabama), Berkeley, Cleveland, Indianapolis, Brockton (Mass.) and Allentown (Penna.). Other communities have programs that combine some features of the special class with regular classroom work. In University City, Missouri, we find "Make-up Classes" and in Dade County, Florida, we find a cross-grouping plan. Pittsburgh, Baltimore and Los Angeles are other cities with some kind of part-time classes for gifted children.

In addition to special full-time or part-time classes for the gifted, we find schools where special emphasis is placed on a more adequate program for gifted students through planned enrichment programs. Portland, Oregon, has acquired a reputation for its efforts on behalf of the gifted by developing activities aimed at helping teachers teach more effectively in regular classrooms. Teachers receive special help in identifying the characteristics of gifted children. They are made conscious of their responsibilities to gifted boys and girls through the work of specialists. They employ teaching materials and procedures varied to meet specific needs of gifted and talented pupils instead of a type of hit-or-miss teaching. Actually what they are doing is making a concerted attempt to guarantee that all gifted and talented boys and girls are challenged to their fullest potentialities.

The Special Class

Enough gifted pupils may be found in some large elementary schools to warrant the establishment of one or more special classes for them in the school. Where the enrollment is small or the number of gifted pupils is limited the children from several schools may be sent to a center where they can work in an ungraded class. The general rule calls for the formation of primary, intermediate and upper grade sections with no more than three grades represented in any one section. A large school may be able to accommodate or fill several classes and thereby narrow the achievement or interest range in regular classrooms, but this is not possible in smaller schools.

Membership in such classes is based on several factors, one of which is intelligence. A minimum IQ of 135 is a prerequisite for placement in some special classes. Hunter College Elementary School has set a minimum IQ requirement of 130, and the Cleveland Major Work Classes require an IQ of 125. Preliminary screenings may be based on group intelligence tests and teacher observation, but final decisions are based on individual tests such as the Stanford-Binet or Wechsler. If the pupil still shows a high potential he may, with the approval of his parents, be placed in the special class.

Consideration is usually given to teacher recommendations, but other special tests, such as achievement tests, aptitude tests, interest inventories and personality tests, may be given to classify pupils. A demonstrated high science potential may be based on the pupil's verbal and mathematics ability. Should he rank high in these two areas, he may become a candidate for further study and ultimate placement in a special class. In general, emotional maturity, social adaptability and physical maturity may be essential factors to be considered in the classification process.

Special class teachers are carefully selected. They work with pupils for the major portion of the day, but special subject teachers may work with the pupils in art, music or foreign language. The basic aim of the special class is to enrich the pupils' lives. Teachers are responsible for increasing the range of knowledge and the perfection of skills in major subject fields. Each teacher tries to stimulate pupils to exceed the normal requirements of a given grade or subject. One of the chief procedures centers around the *development of units*. These may be varied in terms of pupil needs. As they work in small work groups or teams, students engage in projects that have meaning for them. At times they work independently on projects.

Pupils are introduced early to research methods involving short-term, long-term and group research activities as well as independent research activities. Pupil planning and pupil evaluation are considered essential skills that must be learned. Pupil leadership is developed through many unit activities involving committee or team work. Boys and girls learn the meaning of sharing through varied group activities stemming from a planning or conference period. *Discussion* is one of the major methods of sharing ideas and information. Both pupils and teachers report that good discussion techniques are among the most essential aspects of programs for gifted pupils. Each pupil has to learn to think before speaking and to evaluate carefully what has been said during a discussion period. If criticisms are given, they are constructive comments based on recognizing the rights of pupils to differ with opinions stated by other boys and girls.

While many school administrators see the value in special classes for gifted pupils, they still advise bringing children of all classifications together as much as possible.

In some schools this is done by assigning gifted and ungifted children to the same classes for instruction in art, music, physical education, industrial arts and home economics. Some schools operate on the premise that pupils will advance further if they are identified and placed in special classes early, but other schools limit placement in such classes until the pupils reach the intermediate grades. Potentially gifted pupils must complete grade three; then, on the basis of achievement and observed characteristics of giftedness, they are assigned to the "opportunity class" for gifted children.

The underlying philosophy of the special class for the gifted is based on an assumption that boys and girls with superior intellect will be able to complete the work of an average grade in about half the time that average children do. Presumably they are held back in the regular classroom by slower-learning pupils. The goal of the teacher is to help gifted pupils make more effective use of their intellectual powers. She tries to stimulate greater creativity, more self-discipline and better work patterns. The assumption is made that when gifted pupils work with other gifted pupils, they will lose the idea that they are something special. They are forced to exert themselves if they are to hold their own in competing for grades or the attention of the teacher. The pupils engage in enrichment activities that challenge them and extend their knowledge and skill over and beyond what they could be exposed to in the regular classroom competing with average pupils.

The Part-time Special Class

There are a number of school systems with programs calling for attendance in a regular class for a portion of the day, after which time they are excused to take part in special class activities for gifted pupils. These pupils may be in the special classes for a single period, or they may spend half a day in them. The qualifications for attendance in these classes is much the same as for the full-time special classes—although some schools have lowered the minimum IQ to 120. In describing the program offered at University City, Missouri, Norris states that experience has indicated a desirability of a 25- to 35-point difference in the ability of gifted children and average children in a classroom before special consideration is given to the gifted individuals. Consequently, the minimum qualifying intelligence can vary between schools and even between grades of a given school. Here the minimum IQ is never less than 140, with at least 75 per cent of the pupils in the special class having an IQ of above 150. Since an attempt is made at University City to meet individual pupil needs, a gifted pupil with high intelligence may be rejected by the staff if teachers believe that because of social or emotional immaturity he will not benefit from the enrichment program of the Make-up Class.

The Colfax School in Pittsburgh illustrates a special sort of part-time class where gifted children from grades one, two and three make up what is known as the Junior Workshop. Pupils from grades four, five and six make up the Senior Workshop. These pupils spend the equivalent of one-half day in the workshop where they work on academic skills and related enrichment activities. Here pupils work very informally in small groups led by one of their classmates. When they return to regular classes, they tend to work with average pupils in nonacademic subjects such as art, music, science, physical education and library. This is typical of many of the special classes in that the attempt to bring about greater homogeneity is not deemed essential for nonacademic subjects such as art and music.

Due to the shortage of money, teachers and classroom space it is difficult to justify small classes for gifted children. With modern teaching aids and the type of children assigned to special classes, class sizes can be established that have the same teacher-pupil ratio that one finds in average classrooms. Gifted children, for example, have a capacity for independent work as well as a need for leadership responsibility. Both of these factors can lead to much better subgrouping than is often found in average classrooms. Thus, if subgrouping practices are followed, the teacher assigned to work with intellectually gifted or talented children can easily work with more than the number of pupils frequently found in such classes.

Gifted children can come from a single grade or a combination representing a maximum of three or possibly four grade levels. When this is done, the pupils are able to work cooperatively together without reference to grade classifications as such. Due to the differences in the needs and interests of gifted children, the children in the class may be divided into work groups that have some relationship to their special interests or achievement levels. Thus, boys and girls with extra high non-language abilities may receive instruction in areas calling for their type of ability. At the same time they may receive special help in areas where they experience difficulty with high level language skills.

Basically the content of instruction is not considered an essential ingredient. It is merely the vehicle through which children attain the higher goal. They need activities that will help them learn how to search for information. Gifted pupils tend to show greater interest in the *how* and *why* of education than they do in the *what* phase.

Special classes, whether full-time or part-time, provide enrichment in terms of additional subject matter or knowledge, but their chief value lies in the ability to promote greater individual initiative and pupil leadership. The pupils acquire new planning and evaluation skills. They learn the meaning of hard and intensive work. They engage in many research activities, but *discussion techniques* play a very important role in group discussions. Pupils learn to be analytical and critical of each other, so the discussion periods become something more than mere talk. The language arts activities help pupils become more adept at both oral and written expression, especially along creative lines. In many instances field trips, both individual and special-class, become motivating forces leading to intensive study.

In some communities special classes in art, music,

drama, dancing, science or creative writing are held for gifted pupils during nonschool hours. In other communities classes for pupils interested in art or music may be offered by regular teachers after school as "special help" classes or clubs; many of them, however, are offered by other than school personnel. Art classes, for example, are often offered in schools or at museums on Saturday mornings with regular artists as teachers. Many private groups have sponsored special classes for pupils who are interested in the theatre or dancing. In one community a group of writers devoted their efforts to helping children write poetry and short stories. In another community boys and girls attended special ceramics classes. In these special classes interest and talent are prerequisites. Entrance to such activities is not necessarily related to high intelligence and grade lines are nonexistent, so the special enrichment activity may add something to the lives of boys and girls who are not intellectually gifted but who have talent.

Special Classes for the Talented

One form of grouping that has gained some popularity and seems easy to administer consists of bringing together for instruction pupils who have talent in art, music, creative writing, dramatics, science or foreign languages. In one school children who showed talent or strong interest in vocal music or instrumental music were assigned to the same classrooms. This facilitated programing since practice periods and special programs could be held or prepared without upsetting the pupils in other classes with different interests and activities. Children who are assigned to the special talent or interest groups take part in all regular school activities but have some extra time for their particular talent or interest.

One weakness of such programs lies in a tendency to develop a one-sided curriculum for the children. A study of pupil time schedules in one school showed children spending up to one third of their time in music activities. While music activities were helpful to these children, they were *not* receiving a well-balanced program. Many of the more gifted pupils who were in the music classes had other interests but no time for them. Forming classes on the basis of talent did not necessarily mean that intellectually gifted children were brought together because special interests and talents are not always related to intellectual capacity. Although it may be desirable to encourage maximum development of special talent, the curriculum for each pupil should permit maximum growth in all areas, not only in a single field.

The Need for Special Classes

Educators have mixed feelings about the value of a special class for gifted and talented students. In some school systems the school administrator who considers such classes a form of segregation in favor of an elite group does not feel free to oppose those who want something special done for bright children. The idea of a special school or special class appeals to many parents and to many teachers. It may just be a type of halo effect, but a vocal parent group demanding that the board of education take steps to do more for the gifted children in a community cannot be ignored.

In some school systems the issue is never raised because there is no real need for a special class. Children have already been segregated through the formation of homogeneous classes or ability groups. Most of the authorities on the gifted child seem to overlook the fact that a large number of potentially gifted children end up in top-level-ability sections without actually being labeled gifted. Parents whose children are assigned to these regular but special classes take pride in the fact that their progeny are working with a better group of children. In theory at least, the teachers are supposed to be taking the children into learning levels higher than those in the heterogeneously formed classes. Unfortunately, teachers in many of the homogeneously formed classes are assigned a favored group of students but are still limited to the same textbooks and work materials used in regular heterogeneous classes. If there is a difference in the curriculum, it may be considered one of enrichment but with moderation.

In fairness to those who favor special classes for gifted pupils, the point should be made that more planning and study may go into the formation of the special class and in the selection of pupils for such classes than is done for the heterogeneous class. Unfortunately, some of these special classes take on the aura of a private school for public school children, because classes are kept small and children are given an opportunity to express themselves much more freely than in the regular large class. Furthermore, some of the better teachers are assigned to teach the favored children. This factor alone should lead to higher achievement and an improved learning climate. School officials and teachers in one of the nation's bigger cities have admitted that the quality of teaching in some of their regular classes is so poor that it is a wonder the average children learn anything at all. They point to the migration of children from better homes to private and parochial schools as proof that parents want something special for their children. Admittedly, this creates problems for the public schools, but the justification that a special class or special school for the gifted will stem this migration, which has a social basis, is no proof that special classes are the best approach to the problem of gifted children.

Advocates of special classes talk about the values of field trips as broadening experiences. If the thesis can be made that bright children need fewer concrete experiences than slower-learning children, teachers of the less favored children may well argue that their slower-learning children should have the first opportunity to acquire firsthand or concrete experiences. By the same token these teachers can argue that their children are the ones who should be placed in small classes, that their children require more individual attention because they are more dependent upon the teacher than gifted children are. Every list of characteristics of gifted children stresses their ability to learn rapidly and easily, their ability to work independently and to retain what they learn with a minimum of rote drill and other such aids. Still, *small classes and enriched programs* is almost a cliché used by proponents of the special class for the gifted. This raises the question, which few educators are ready to answer, about the real need for the special class. Would special classes for gifted children really be necessary if all children were assigned to small classes with the guarantee that well-trained, experienced and capable teachers who have the primary interests of the pupils at heart would carry out programs based on the children's levels of achievement, needs and interests?

If the special class is an escape from an impossible situation for a selected group of children, those responsible for our schools are not facing up to their responsibilities. This is what makes evaluation of special programs difficult. Justification for a special program for gifted children is apt to be made on the basis of a comparison between a poor learning climate and one approaching the ideal. The result in such cases can be foreordained. The problem is essentially one of comparing the achievements of pupils in the special class with the achievements of comparable children left in regular classrooms where all children received the benefits of small class size, an enriched program and good teaching.

Evaluation of Special Classes for Gifted Children

Any attempt to show the value of special programs for gifted pupils must be limited because there is a lack of measuring instruments to support the argument that through these special programs children have become more creative, have learned to assume leadership roles or have learned to work independently. These values are highly desirable, so it would help if positive proof could be produced to justify the conclusion that pupils have indeed become more critical and more creative. The absence of such tests limits the defense of the special program to highly subjective statements by teachers, consultants, parents and pupils, such as the following:

> The whole-class plan has been a successful way of challenging gifted children academically and guiding their growth socially. Their satisfied, enthusiastic manner is reflected in their behavior and growth.

This teacher had spent a year with a gifted class. She had enjoyed her work because she had been given the freedom to take the children as far as their interests took them. She admits that she learned to appreciate the tremendous resources her ten- and eleven-year-olds possessed, but she had nothing concrete to show for her statement that the whole-class plan had been a successful way to challenge gifted children.

In another school system the gifted-class teachers said they thought their efforts had been beneficial to all the boys and girls assigned to them. While their statements were not positive, they were less vague and subjective than some because they did have the support of achievement tests. These tests showed that their first grade pupils attained greater growth in reading and arithmetic than the students in the controlled group who had not had the advantage of the special class.

Unfortunately, there are a number of variables that make it difficult to accept even the evidence of achievement tests.

1. *Motivation.* Even when matched pairs are compared in a special class and regular classroom situation, it is difficult to overlook the fact that pupils assigned to the special class may be more highly motivated. For example, in the selective process the pupil who volunteers may be more highly motivated because of initiative, ambition, curiosity or parental support. His parents may be the

ones who favored the program and supported a drive to have him accepted. Thus, two pupils with identical intelligence quotients may not make equal progress because of the difficulty in controlling the forces that make one gifted pupil strive to reach higher goals while another equally talented pupil is content to remain an underachiever.

2. *The Hawthorne Effect.* It is difficult to assess the impact of some special programs because of the Hawthorne Effect. The mere fact that students and teachers are part of a program that is different becomes a motivating factor. Teachers make an extra effort and pupils take extra pains to do a good job if they are conscious that they are being watched. Moreover parents of the children in the special program are quite apt to promote activities at home that will help their sons and daughters realize desired goals in school.

3. *Opinions.* The opinion poll is generally based on asking parents, teachers and pupils their reactions to a special program. The responses are often general and highly subjective because many of those questioned lack background from which to draw a sound conclusion and others will be somewhat prejudiced in favor of a program that gives them or their children something extra. In the case of teachers many of them will find it easier to teach small classes of bright children than to teach average or below-average learners in less favored learning situations. Here again, being part of a new program is quite likely to give the teacher a positive outlook on her work.

4. *The teacher variable.* Few school administrators will begin a new program without consciously or unconsciously stacking the deck in favor of its being a successful endeavor by assigning experienced—even their most alert or promising—teachers. However, studies have shown that individual differences on the part of gifted pupils can affect the quality of the work they do with different teachers. The teachers may be outstanding, but their approaches to a particular class and its needs may bring about results other than those desired. If compatibility could be anticipated the results of a year of close

working relationships would be much different from what happens when it is ignored.

5. *Rapid achievement.* The fact that students in a special gifted class make a gain of two to three academic years' growth in the normal school year cannot be accepted as proof that the special program is a success because bright pupils are quite likely to make such growth, at least in the field of reading, without benefit of their segregation from a more heterogeneous group.

6. *Test inadequacies.* The test used for average children may have too low a ceiling to show true growth for the superior student. Also, different tests will not always be comparable with regularly selected tests. For example, the grade equivalent obtained on an Iowa Test of Basic Skills does not indicate the same type of growth that can be represented in the composite score made on the Stanford or the Metropolitan achievement tests. Many potential growth areas attributed to the new program are still difficult to evaluate although some new tests are being used to measure such things as personality changes, critical thinking and creative growth.

7. *The class environment.* The gifted classes may not be any smaller in size than regular classes; however, if they are smaller, the pupils are immediately given an advantage that can upset any attempt to show superior growth in academic or nonacademic areas. Frequently the pupils in the special class have the advantage of new and additional textbooks, supplementary learning devices and library books, plus a number of audiovisual aids and a few field trips. Where the class environment is changed perceptibly, the climate for learning is no longer comparable so the potential gains may be due to factors other than those of segregation.

8. *Balance of sexes.* In some schools the attempt to form a more homogeneous group or a so-called class of top or gifted children is based on a combination of achievement and intelligence scores. This can result in an imbalance of the sexes because of the reading factor. Compared with girls of equal intellect many bright boys

do not read as fast or with as much comprehension; therefore, the special class may be automatically weighted in favor of an accelerated growth in reading.

9. *Teaching techniques.* What happens in the new classroom will often depend upon what teachers teach and how or when they teach a given topic. For example, superior students will often continue to show rapid growth in reading because they read widely at home as well as in school but these same pupils may show little if any growth in arithmetic. There may be many reasons for this, one of which is the teacher's technique. If the teacher attempts to teach her whole class new arithmetic skills, she limits the growth of those who may already be proficient in those skills. These pupils will show little extra growth if they have to wait for the teacher to introduce them to the new arithmetic experiences because they are less likely to obtain the same type of extra practice in arithmetic as in reading supplemented at home by their own reading interests. If the teacher limits her teaching to the same established curriculum and materials used with average learners, some of the advantage of the special grouping will be lost. Her bright pupils would be much better off if she used different materials or at least minimized the use of learning exercises that are merely review for pupils who are ready for higher learning.

Many teachers, principals and parents are convinced that the assignment of pupils to a special class or school is the ultimate answer to problems encountered by gifted children; however, the proof that desired objectives can be realized by such action is very difficult to obtain. Studies of the accomplishments of exceptionally bright pupils in various communities have shown that great gains have been made by some of the segregated students in one or more academic subjects, especially reading; however, in other communities the results have not been as positive. Students have not achieved as much success in arithmetic in some of the schools where reading growth was most satisfying. In other communities anticipated growth has not been evident. This lack of accelerated growth on the part of older underachieving gifted students is the result of their inability to modify their poor work-study patterns readily after years of frustrating activities from work habits not conducive to high-level learning activities. There is a growing suspicion that delayed identification of gifted children can limit the growth of such individuals once they have reached adolescence and must begin to make decisions in the face of conflicting pressures; for example, the desire to be popular with peermates, the desire to be independent, to have a car, a boat or a boy friend. Mere placement in a special class for high school subjects may not be sufficient motivation to overcome outside pressures or negative work-study habits.

5 *Meeting Needs Through Acceleration*

Each year thousands of new books, magazines, pamphlets and research studies are printed, but even intellectually curious individuals can sample only a minute portion of the available material. Most adults do not have time to read widely because they get involved in problems of living, or if they read, they do so in selected areas related to special interest and needs. Many of these adults admit that they wish they had read more widely in school because there are so many fields in which they find themselves unprepared or incompetent. One has only to look at the vast number of adults who return to school to build up areas of weakness or to study in new fields to see that a narrow curriculum is not enough for life in our modern, complex society. This should indicate the need to offer all children and especially gifted pupils a richer and broader curriculum. Yet there are parents and educators who believe that the schools are not doing their job unless they rush superior or gifted pupils through school.

Many of them believe that the ability to finish a book or course in less than a year is cause for acceleration based upon the concept of skipping grades. Why have a bright pupil stay with the regular class when he can finish reading a book or can master skills before most of the other pupils have even started?

Justification for grade skipping lies in the traditional grade standard concept of education. Here the teacher works with limited materials and has to hold back gifted pupils because she cannot introduce new skills or subject matter reserved for the next grade. In such schools the superior pupils are not challenged, so there is support for allowing them to skip a grade. If success in school is measured in terms of narrow ranges of achievement, gifted children can easily skip a grade or two without difficulty since they will always find themselves entering classes which have a large number of pupils who have been progressing through school at a normal rate of speed but who are not always ready for the learning skills taught in class. In a short time most gifted pupils catch up with these slower learning students and then forge ahead again. Research studies have indicated that skipping grades is not harmful to gifted pupils; however, they tend to emphasize acceleration through traditional schools and not modern schools where children can take part in a broad and enriching series of activities when they have completed the basic minimum requirements of a grade or class.

If one is merely measuring ability to achieve in prescribed traditional academic subjects, there is no question that the gifted pupil can "hold his own" in high school or college where he is still competing with pupils of lesser ability. However, this type of education should not be considered sufficient for life in the modern world, no matter how bright a pupil is at the elementary or junior high school level. He should be reading some of the new materials coming off the presses and reading in depth about the background or causes of past and present events. Furthermore, because there are many areas of study teachers do not have time to touch or dwell upon, gifted pupils can use many valuable hours acquiring additional skills and new knowledge if they complete the minimum program ahead of schedule without actually skipping grades.

There is no need for skipping grades where teachers are free to teach new skills or new bodies of knowledge whenever they find pupils are ready to go on to new learning levels. Here, there is no leveling off of learning for the superior student; hence, gifted pupils are not permitted to stagnate, to coast, to get bored or to fall into poor study habits. With all the sources of learning which can be made available for rapid learners, these students can be challenged without acceleration through skipping.

When pupils *are* accelerated through skipping grades, they are able to complete the traditional school in a shorter span of time. However, there may be breaks in their education if succeeding teachers fail to make an attempt to fill gaps in their background. This often happens when pupils are introduced to new subjects having a definite relationship to skills introduced in the regular grade which the accelerated student has missed. Although very bright pupils can overcome their apparent deficiencies, they often encounter difficulties that can be frustrating. If the objective is to get these pupils into college at sixteen or seventeen, the same results can be achieved by accelerating the curriculum rather than the pupil. With planned curriculum acceleration the problem of skipping important sequences or skills disappears. Educators who believe that early entrance into college is a prerequisite for gifted pupils may give serious thought to the values of planned acceleration as a substitute for "grade skipping."

Many parents and educators subscribe to a philosophy which is supported by Terman and Oden who stated that boys and girls with IQ's of 130 or above "should be promoted sufficiently to permit college entrance by the age of seventeen at the latest." Actually, they indicated a belief that "a majority in this group would be better off to enter at sixteen." Apparently there is a widespread belief that gifted pupils have learned all there is to know at lower grade levels, so they must be rushed into college at early chronological ages. This goal can be realized without actually skipping grades if the curriculum is accelerated to the point that each pupil is allowed to make continuous progress in terms of his own ability to advance to higher stages of learning.

Studies on Acceleration by Skipping

There has been considerable research regarding the effects, advantages and disadvantages of acceleration. While the tenor of this research would indicate that there are advantages to the gifted pupil, it must be recognized that the studies tend to report pupil success in schools where there *was a lockstep education*, where boys and girls were not considered as individuals free to expand both horizontally as well as vertically in a planned accelerated program. One must question research that ignores the need to develop well-rounded individuals—boys and girls who know their mathematics, science and foreign languages, but who know also their art, music, literature and history. All too often college-bound students are burdened by academic pressures and do not have free time for experimental reading, wide discussion, attendance at plays, participation in sports and other important activities.

However, several studies were published in the thirties that supported acceleration by skipping. Keys negated the argument that gifted pupils do not have time to live. This study of graduates from Oakland, California, high schools indicated that the younger students took more scholarship honors, took part in more activities and were elected to more class offices than comparable pupils in their controlled group. Furthermore, the accelerated students showed less timidity and shyness. Two studies by Engle reported no appreciable effect on the personal adjustment of students in the larger high schools of Indiana. This was substantiated by Wilkins' report that scholastic achievement and social adjustment were unaffected by acceleration. Gray's report evaluated the accomplishments of 126 boys and 28 girls who entered college while they were under sixteen years of age. He shows that these pupils excelled in every point of comparison, namely intelligence, scholarship, health, physical growth, extracurricular activities and social adjustment. McConnell reported on the success of Cornell students who had only three years of high school. He found that scholastic ability rather than age or years of previous schooling seemed to be the key to the success of these students.

Some twenty years later studies were still coming up with the same results. In 1953 and 1954 Justman reported on the social and personal adjustment of a group of pupils who completed a three-year junior high school program in two years. These reports indicated that the younger pupils were slightly better adjusted from a personal and social standpoint than the nonaccelerated pupils. In 1962, Mirman's study of 128 Los Angeles seniors, half of whom had accelerated, revealed no difference in the social adjustment of those who had moved through school rapidly in comparison with those who had gone through it at the normal pace. This study also points out that the accelerated group took a more active part in the sports program than those carrying lighter academic loads.

In all these studies and many more, the evidence seems to point up the fact that gifted children can make necessary adjustments when they have skipped grades. If there are bad effects, they seem to be found where pupils are not actually gifted students.

Programs sponsored by the Fund of the Advancement of Education have met with similar success. Their Program for Early Admission to College gave scholarships to students who were sixteen-and-a-half years old when they entered college. These bright students had not completed high school, but they were consistently able to outperform their classmates in academic work. They also reportedly made better academic progress than students in a nonaccelerated controlled group who had comparable ability. The adjustment problems by two pupils were little different from those encountered by nonaccelerated pupils who had social and emotional problems. This success led to the development of the Program for Admission to College with Advanced Standing. Students were encouraged to take college credit courses in high school. Studies showed that gifted high school pupils could meet college requirements and hold their own as advanced students in college. This led to the adoption in 1956 of the Advanced Placement Program which has been accepted by many colleges.

Experiments in Acceleration

While studies have been justifying acceleration by skipping, experiments have been successfully carried out in planned acceleration. R. H. Braun reported on experiments in which superior ninth grade students at Urbana High School were urged to take biology instead of general science. To do so the pupils had to obtain a *B-plus* grade in their eighth grade general science. At the end of the year the freshmen took the Cooperative Biology Test. The median score for the accelerated pupils was at the 90th percentile and was much higher than the median score of the sophomores, juniors and seniors who took the same test.

As a result of the success in accelerating ninth graders into biology, other students were accelerated into advanced classes at Urbana. Seventh graders who had done outstanding work in arithmetic were permitted to substitute algebra for eighth grade arithmetic. Other students who had done outstanding work in seventh grade English classes were permitted to take ninth grade English in place of eighth grade English. Students who did well in seventh grade science classes were permitted to take ninth grade science in place of eighth grade science. Placement in these accelerated courses was based on school marks and achievement and aptitude tests, with parental approval.

At North Arlington, New Jersey, selected eighth graders took algebra with ninth graders. This was done on the basis of their prior achievement in arithmetic classes, the results of the Iowa Basic Test in Arithmetic and teacher recommendations, as well as evaluation on a mathematics readiness test. At the end of the algebra course it was discovered that the accelerated algebra pupils received most of the high grades given out by the teachers. The study showed that no accelerated pupil received a single mark below a *B* and a number of them received *A's*. The eighth grade marks were in the top 20 per cent of all the algebra marks given out in the course of the year. A similar result was obtained when eighth graders, on the basis of past performance in regular classes and intellectual ability, took first-year French on an elective basis.

New York City has two programs for gifted junior high school pupils. One group of students has been allowed to accelerate the normal three-year program in two years. This should not, however, be considered in the same light as skipping grades since their programs were planned to avoid leaving gaps in the students' backgrounds. A second group of gifted pupils works through the three-year junior high school curriculum without saving a chronological year. Their extra time is filled with a broad program of enrichment activities.

Students have done very well in such accelerated programs. Bright pupils do not have too much trouble finding their place on an academic level in a subject normally given at upper grade levels. This is especially true if activities offered at an advanced level are in only limited sequence with activities that would normally have been engaged in at a preceding grade level. This type of acceleration permits brighter pupils (1) to broaden their general background because they are permitted to take a less restrictive program; having gained from one to three units of high school credit in required fields, they can select electives in fields of their own interest; (2) to graduate from high school early; or (3) to elect to remain in high school as advanced students, taking advanced courses that carry college credit. In the last case the gifted students continue to take part in broadening and exciting activities with their peers in chronological age. Conceivably, they can enter college with from 15 to 20 hours of advanced credit.

Further support of acceleration comes from a report on pupils who were able to start school earlier than is customary. This type of acceleration has merit, but it is often fraught with controversy. Hobson reported in 1947 on a study, spanning fifteen years, of children who had been entered in kindergarten at an early chronological age. These children who had high mental ages at entry had no difficulty as they went through the primary grades. They adjusted both physically and academically and were less frequently referred to counselors for personal, emotional or social problems. These findings were substantiated by Worcester in 1955, who reported on children who entered kindergarten eight months early as a result of intelligence test findings. These pupils made good social adjustments and were all accepted by their peers as they went through the primary grades.

Numerous school systems have adopted the policy of admitting gifted boys and girls a year earlier than usual on the basis of special examinations. The results of a Stanford-Binet test or Wechsler plus social and emotional maturity have been used to accelerate these children through early admission into kindergarten.

A program of planned acceleration in a Mineola, New York, elementary school was based on the continuation of school for a group of elementary school children through an extra month of school in the summer. Children selected for the study from the fourth grade were grouped homogeneously for three full years plus four summers. At the end of the period it was found that they had gained one year academically on the California Achievement Test. They caught up with a control group that had been one year ahead of them academically at the start of the study and moved one year beyond another controlled group of pupils who had not been allowed to accelerate.

Secondary school pupils in high schools all over the country have also benefited from summer courses. These have been setting the stage for a type of acceleration by offering advanced level courses. With credit received for such summer courses, boys and girls have been able to accelerate through high school.

An experiment in one school system demonstrates the way in which acceleration can be planned to help make it successful in meeting the needs of gifted pupils. Pupils are carefully studied as they go through the primary grades. At the end of the third grade the parents of rapidly progressing children are invited to a conference. They are told that the teachers consider that their child appears eligible for placement in a special fourth grade enrichment program that could lead to placement in the sixth grade instead of the fifth. If parents object to the planned acceleration, the matter is dropped and the child in question is assigned to a regular fourth grade. Where parents and teachers agree on the wisdom of the special enrichment year, the pupils work with their fourth grade teacher at advanced levels and in an enriched program to ensure that they will not miss any important phase of work normally covered in the fifth grade. If the pupils continue to work up to teacher expectations, they move into regular sixth grade classes without actually spending any time in the fifth grade.

To be eligible for the planned acceleration program a pupil must have an IQ of 120 and must be at least two years above grade level in reading and one year above grade level in arithmetic. In addition to the performance on standardized tests, consideration is given to the actual classroom achievement of each individual. These achievement reports are supplemented by teacher observations. A check list may be used to show emotional, social and physical maturity. A composite report may be based upon the use of sociometric tests, parent conferences over a number of years plus recommendations from regular and special teachers.

While there may be some variation in the requirements for a pre-planned acceleration program, the pattern will be similar to the one described above. Studies have been made which indicate that children who have taken part in a pre-planned type of grade skipping can make a good adjustment to their new classmates and the program offered in the new grade. Unfortunately, there is one problem that continues to trouble those responsible for the gifted child acceleration program, and that is the apparent failure to identify all gifted and talented children in time to place them in the special program. This is frequently evident in the test results of high achieving students who fail to meet designated group and individual intelligence prerequisites, yet who continue to obtain test scores in the eighty-fifth or higher percentile rank. Nothing special is done for these individuals, yet they continue to work at such high levels that one can only conclude that the criteria for placement in an acceleration class for gifted children need to be reviewed.

Planned Acceleration in the Ungraded School

The curriculum of the ungraded elementary school allows pupils to progress at their own rates of speed. The curriculum is accelerated for pupils who are ready to take part in higher-level activities without having to wait for promotion to the next grade. They engage in a continuous series of learning activities based upon readiness for the next stage of learning and the ability to succeed in related subject fields. Bright pupils in an ungraded primary school can easily master the reading skills in less than the normal three years. Some bright pupils may conceivably be ready to start fourth grade reading activities at the end of what would be considered the second grade without having actually skipped a year if they are allowed to work through a series of sequential learning steps at an accelerated pace. If the intermediate grade classes are ungraded, these same pupils can conceivably enter seventh grade after a second stint of concentrated work. Thus, a truly gifted pupil would be able to cover the equivalent of six elementary grades in the space of four chronological years. Although he is still young chronologically and socially, he may be ready to do the academic work normally taught in the seventh grade. Here the pupil has been accelerated by being able to work steadily through a fixed curriculum at his own pace. If he has trouble at one level, he spends more time mastering the essential skills needed for the next step and is meanwhile free to make up for his lost time by proceeding more rapidly in areas where he had no need for special help and was able to develop proficiency faster than his peers.

Curriculum Acceleration
Through Subgrouping

Teachers in graded schools can achieve the same results as the teachers in the schools designated as ungraded through subgrouping and an agreement that each teacher will truly take children where she finds them. This means that teachers will work with slow learners at lower grade learning levels while they work with rapid learners at advanced levels. In this situation grades become meaningless if the curriculum is thought of in terms of identifiable skills and bodies of knowledge. Pupils should be able to move at their own rates of speed as long as they can apply their knowledge or skill to solve realistic problems. In many instances the pupils are ready to move on to higher levels of learning in the regular classroom, but artificial barriers tend to hold them back. Teachers can enrich the curriculum for many pupils, but this is not always the answer.

Planned acceleration by dropping some phases of upper grade skills or areas of study to lower grade lines is better than skipping pupils. Through curriculum acceleration the fast-learning pupils continue to work with pupils who are supposedly on their same chronological age and social plane. Each pupil works at his own pace with a subgroup in a subject field. He may be accelerated in some phases of the curriculum where he has special interest or aptitudes while he is working at normal grade levels in others. In very small schools some cross-grade and multiclass groupings may be desirable to bring together enough fast-learning pupils to form a teachable group in a particular subject. In some cases individual pupils who have progressed through the first four grades at a continuous and rapid pace may be allowed to bypass a grade such as the fifth without any perceptible loss or handicap since in such a program he will have mastered a sequence of studies that included what is normally taught at the fifth grade level.

Grade Skipping Versus Planned Acceleration

Numerous studies have shown that gifted boys and girls can complete the normal elementary and secondary school curriculums in less than the traditional thirteen years. As a rule they can find success in college if their acceleration has not exceeded more than two chronological years or grades; however, many teachers and school administrators are opposed to acceleration programs as a matter of principle. They will argue that the accelerated students will not be mature enough, but beyond this generalization they tend to get lost in vague generalities that have been refuted time and again.

While many of these same educators will oppose any plan to skip the equivalent of a standard grade, a large number of them accept the principle of nongraded schooling which carries with it the assumption that gifted or rapid learners will move through school unhampered by traditional grade restrictions. Unfortunately, this does not seem to carry through in practice. Many pupils who complete a normal reading program in two years instead of three find administrative barriers that prevent their taking full advantage of the acceleration movement started in the primary grades. To date very few schools have allowed the nongraded concept to extend into the junior or senior high school.

Nongraded programs carry with them the connotation that children will progress continuously through a program of study without actually leaving out any learning stages. In the traditional school which used grade skipping as a form of acceleration, this was not true. The seventh grade student who was suddenly entering high school as a ninth grader often found that he had to make some adjustments due to the lack of those introductory weeks of algebra that most eighth graders had prior to graduation.

The concept of advanced placement in college is based on the thesis that students will acquire a full background of skills and knowledge in high school or in courses offered on a college campus to special high school students. This type of acceleration is quite popular with gifted high school students, but it may be questioned in terms of the direction of the student's academic growth. Did the student elect vertical growth when some phases of horizontal growth would have helped to round out his total background? This question cannot be readily answered because studies have not shown the contrast between students who have elected to accelerate through high school instead of taking part in a full program of broadening activities.

In view of the advanced achievement in many subject areas, gifted boys and girls are finding traditional high school courses an insult to their intelligence. This is where nongraded high school courses would help many of the high achieving gifted students explore new high school courses as well as take advanced placement courses. For example, placement in upper grade classes may be opened to freshmen and sophomores on the basis of qualifying examinations. Achievement would then become a criterion for acceptance in a regular high school course instead of chronological years of schooling. Even under this program intellectually gifted students would find themselves running out of courses, so the ultimate end would still be acceleration, but without many of the frustrations encountered in present programs.

6 Meeting Needs Through Enrichment

Many teachers favor a school organizational plan that places children together on a chronological age basis. Under such a program there is no acceleration of students who have special talents. Individual differences are to be provided for through subgrouping activities and a very broad enrichment program. Democratic living becomes a key word as slow, average and gifted children work together in a social situation that recognizes no barriers. The classroom, in a manner of speaking, becomes lifelike in that it represents the broader community or the world children will live in when they leave school. In such a classroom the true leaders will have a chance to grow and find themselves.

While educators are not in accord with this philosophy some studies have shown the value of mixing gifted children with nongifted children. This does not mean that learning for the gifted will be kept at the same level as it is for the slower progressing students, but by being in the same classroom, the gifted and talented children bring an element that cannot be replaced when they are in homogeneous classes with intelligence or reading achievement the criterion for segregating the students.

Average pupils lose leaders and helpers when gifted pupils are taken from the regular class. Frequently, these better-than-average students are the ones who set the stage for exciting class activities. Because they can complete normal assignments in a short time, they have the time to spend on activities of an enrichment nature. This means that they can bring new and exciting things to a class. They may share a book, story, poem or art masterpiece that lightens the day for everyone including the teacher. Through their activity or their example the whole class can be motivated to new projects, tasks or assignments.

Many teachers have found that some projects would never get under way without the drive and enthusiasm of gifted or bright pupils. These pupils are apt to see what is wanted and can get things moving because they are interested or curious. They are often the ones who help make learning valuable to others and in turn are themselves stimulated to greater exertions in the role of leader. Because of their initiative the day-by-day routine of the textbook is often eliminated. They can help liven the round table discussion, make displays, paint murals, plan dramatic presentations or conduct experiments. From many small-group activities the teacher finds the impetus leading to large-group or all-class activities. Thus, many all-class projects stem from activities started by gifted children. Frequently, they engage in enrichment activities that prove so interesting that nongifted children beg for an opportunity to engage in similar types of activities. As a result we may find teachers holding back bright pupils because they know that the other children will want to follow in their footsteps. In such cases the teachers are missing a rare opportunity to motivate their children to work at higher levels to realize their potential.

Studies show that teaching and learning tend to improve for all students when teachers make special provisions for gifted children in the classroom. At the same time the gifted children benefit from the opportunity to share their experiences and from acting the true role of a leader. They have an opportunity to grow in areas lost to them when they are placed in selected classes made up entirely of intellectually gifted children. While there may be intellectual advantages in such classes, many leadership opportunities are apt to be nonexistent.

Another argument for keeping gifted students in the regular classroom is that all pupils do not have the same interest and drive. As a result one finds gifted children who need the stability that comes with working with average pupils. They cannot continue to work at a steady pace. This may be especially true if they are creative. They need time to think, explore and work at a level where they can enjoy life without pressure.

Many bright pupils find contentment in being a member of a steady, stable group. They need to work with other pupils who have similar interests and who can find success in activities they enjoy. These bright pupils find contentment in being part of a group where they do not have to stretch themselves. They do not want to be scholars. There are many educators who believe that it is wrong to allow bright children to become satisfied with what they call mediocrity, but considering the unhappiness in the world and the large number of physical breakdowns each year it may be better to give these pupils a good rich background of experiences in an atmosphere where they can find both challenge and contentment.

Those who hold this point of view favor greater emphasis on enrichment as well as subgrouping and a planned curriculum of acceleration. With such school policies gifted boys and girls will not be slowed academically as they have been in the traditional school organization. At the same time they and their average classmates benefit from common activities on their social and emotional level. Mere acceleration of children through the traditional curriculum should not be considered adequate to meet the basic needs of either average learners or those classified as rapid and gifted learners.

The Nature of Enrichment

The word *enrichment* indicates that something extra is added to a program for selected pupils. Actually, every pupil should have the right to take part in a wide variety of enriching activities in terms of his capacities and achievement levels. If this philosophy is accepted, the resulting curriculum should appeal to all pupils regardless of whether they fall into the slow, average or gifted category. For instance, the field trip is not considered an activity that should be limited to gifted children in a special class; instead it is an integral part of the program for all children because of the wide stimulation and motivation such an activity can promote. Each pupil, if properly guided, will get something out of the field trip commensurate with what he puts into it. In other words, the field trip can become a basic part of a program in a regular classroom with the expectation that gifted pupils will play a leadership role in helping to plan, organize and evaluate the activity.

In one school a group of eighth grade pupils reviewed their experiences in the lower grades. Three boys spoke highly about trips to the opera, to the fish hatchery, to the United Nations Building and to the State Museum as highlights they would never forget. Two of their peers who had been assigned to classes stripped of the gifted children spoke bitterly about a program that had never included class trips because their teachers had said they could not afford the time from regular classroom activities to go gallivanting around the countryside. This may have been jealousy but it represents a problem in that one group of children engages in activities denied to others. This type of situation should not develop if the values of field trips are understood by teachers because all pupils would take part in such activities.

In another school the gifted pupils were given the responsibility of planning a number of special activities for the class long before a particular study was to be undertaken. Two of the pupils made a special study of the water works that supplied the community with water. They visited the Water Department to interview an engineer, secure literature and arrange for a class trip to the water purification plant. The two pupils made reports to their class on their findings, led discussions and helped set the stage for the actual trip. Every pupil benefited from the pupil specialty, which gave life to their study of an important phase of life in their community.

The foregoing pupil activities could be considered forms of enrichment activities but teachers working with the students considered them only one phase of a total program for growing boys and girls. Leadership opportunities were created and many students took advantage of the situations to go far beyond the ordinary demands of the grade. Gifted pupils were able to go further than some of their less capable classmates, but through stimulation of activities that went beyond the traditional textbook approach, there were average boys and girls who spent long hours at home preparing reports, charts and other illustrative materials to make their committee activity a success. They did this willingly because the enrichment activities had helped make ordinary studies meaningful.

Good enrichment activities supplement the basic program in many schools without receiving too much publicity while in other schools enrichment is hardly understood. In such schools the gifted child and the average child alike find everyday school routine becomes quite dull after a time. In thousands of classrooms one finds enrichment is limited because of poor teaching techniques, overlarge class enrollments, rigid curriculums and a dearth of textbooks, library books and essential references that would supplement the basic texts.

As mentioned earlier, Portland, Oregon, is one of the few communities that has received considerable publicity for its attempts to meet the needs of gifted students through an enrichment program in the regular classroom. The whole school system has become gifted-minded. Children have been identified in terms of their capacities, and special help in the form of enrichment activities has been recommended to the teachers. The program is under the direction of an able administrator who works with a number of assistants, including extra teachers who help meet the needs of gifted children by working directly with the teachers and the pupils.

Examples of Enrichment Activities for Gifted Elementary School Children

Enrichment activities may be provided in all classrooms for all children, but many of them will have special meaning for those who fall into the gifted category. Some of the following activities have been used successfully to stimulate pupils to continue their growth without acceleration.

1. To stimulate pupils with ability to write, teachers encouraged them to keep a log or diary. Pupils were also encouraged to develop hobbies that help them acquire a better understanding of the world and its resources. In one school a philatelist visited the classes to help organize a Stamp Club, which proved extremely helpful in the fields of history and geography.

2. Bright pupils at the upper grade level were permitted to take part in a recreational reading or leisure-time reading class in place of the regular reading class. These pupils were required to account for their time and activity, but they worked without supervision. The pupils read widely and reportedly explored areas they would not have come in contact with had they remained in the regular class. They rotated pupil supervisors most successfully and thereby freed the teacher to work two periods a week with other children who needed assistance in reading skill areas.

3. One teacher encouraged children to write stories, limericks, poems and articles, which were collected and edited by the students. A group of pupils typed and mimeographed the best samples of their creative work during the first half of the school year. The students bound the selected writings and sold copies to pupils in other grades and classes where they led to considerable

discussion and became the basis for study and learning by pupils of all abilities.

4. Pupils with a flair for dramatizing were given an opportunity to write a skit or mock radio program. The students put their own programs on the air via the loudspeaker, or they put on productions for other classes in the assembly. One group of pupils relieved teachers from noon duty on bad-weather days by putting on skits or dramatic presentations in the gymnasium for the children who could not go out on the playground for a few minutes after lunch.

5. Children who are interested in dramatics can be encouraged to read plays, study techniques for making television productions, motion pictures and regular stage productions. Students can do considerable reading research as well as cultural research. As a culminating activity the students may give dramatic readings to children in their class or other classes or they may present a play. In one school interested mothers worked with the children after school in order to learn stage techniques, the art of makeup, voice projection and role play. At least once a year these bright children planned, secured costumes, made stage settings and put on a play for the benefit of the parents in the community.

6. One group of fifth grade pupils took primary grade children to the library for story hours. Here they dramatized or read stories to the younger children. Children are introduced to the resources of the library and are taught the use of the card catalog, encyclopedias, yearbooks, the thesaurus and other reference materials. Less capable children do not get acquainted with the library until much later.

7. Pupils assumed the responsibility for arranging bulletin boards or displays in corridor display cabinets on a monthly schedule. They worked with art teachers, regular classroom teachers and pupils from different grades in the preparation of special materials, models, pictures and samples of pupil work.

8. Many students were encouraged to develop science

interests by making collections such as rocks, soil, minerals and seeds. Others took school or community problems as the basis for detailed studies or projects. Students made models of their water supply or waste disposal plant to show how the community serves the people.

9. Students constructed arithmetic puzzles similar to crossword puzzles for use in teaching the meaning of arithmetic terms. One group of intermediate grade boys made arithmetic teaching aids for use in primary grades.

10. Gifted pupils developed specialties that allowed them to become resource people on special projects for their own class or for other classes.

11. Children may use many supplementary books written on an advanced level to challenge and stimulate their thinking and actions. Pupils learned how to evaluate a book and report on their findings.

12. Many musically inclined students find enjoyment in writing original tunes and lyrics. Boys and girls may take tape recordings of class or group activities for analysis and reports. Tape recordings may be made for a presentation to visiting parents. Special programs for class presentation may be made through use of the tape recorder.

13. Children may write articles for a class or school newspaper. In one school the fifth and sixth graders were able to prepare a column of school news for the local newspaper. They collected and edited all the stories that were printed. Intermediate grade students may learn to serve as group or class reporters. They record comments, questions and important data and make brief summaries of what has happened during a work session or discussion. Children may also write letters to children in other states or countries. Boys and girls can interview interesting people in the community for information not given in standard sources of information.

14. Pupils with science interests may set up experiments or conduct demonstrations for teachers who may not be as adept in the handling of science equipment or material.

15. Murals may be planned cooperatively and then

developed by individuals or teams. Pupils may work independently or collectively in the designing of posters for a worthy cause—for example, a safety poster or health poster. Pupils may make models or scale drawings to illustrate stages in the development of inventions such as the cotton gin, the automobile and the airplane. They may be used to illustrate a theme such as the story of transportation on land, on the water or in the air. Dioramas may be made involving use of the models.

16. Pupils have learned how to use the slide rule in the intermediate grades.

17. Pupils have made special studies of children's interests in nonschool hours. One group made an evaluation of television programs. A second group made an intensive study of comic books and reported their findings to pupils in other classes.

18. Advanced-level arithmetic books may be used by some pupils to allow given individuals to continue working with the class but at an advanced level.

19. Pupils may learn how to make and dress puppets and then use them to tell a story. They may write a play for a puppet show, build a stage or theater and put on special programs for other boys and girls.

20. Selected students may visit other classes and grades in a school. In some school systems a student exchange between schools has been encouraged.

21. Science corners have been developed and maintained entirely by interested pupils. Foreign languages for gifted pupils may be introduced at the primary or intermediate grade level. Pupils may start with a conversational language approach. Elementary school children may begin to study the concepts of sets and their application to elementary school arithmetic.

22. Pupils who are not very adept mechanically may go to a special classroom in a school or even another school to learn how to use and care for simple tools.

23. Pupils learn to prepare outlines to guide themselves and others in making reports.

24. Pupils may make special maps to show historical

events. Lower grade pupils may want to make a map showing only centers of interest in their community.

25. Boys and girls may plan an imaginary trip to a distant national park or center of interest. They can plan the whole trip in terms of routes, cost, time, possible obstacles and side trips that can be taken en route.

26. Pupils may look up rules for games and teach others how to play them. One group made up a small book of rules and directions for games they liked to play.

27. Pupils may make up comparison budgets showing cost of living today and yesterday.

28. Girls in one school made up a dance. It was completely original and the intricate steps were most effective as they dramatized a scene from history through dancing.

29. Pupils may plan an airplane or train trip requiring the ability to read and use a timetable.

30. Pupils may organize school drives for worthy causes or projects in the school or community.

31. Girls may enjoy serving as relief assistants to kindergarten and first grade teachers and learning how to work with young children. They learn how to read to young children and to supervise them in class or playground activities.

32. Children may set up book displays for other teachers or for the librarian.

33. Pupils may use the tape recorder to study their own speech patterns or those of others. Pupils may read a story and then try to add new incidents or endings to it. Pupils may also engage in debates or discussions in their class or with pupils from upper grade classes.

34. Intermediate grade children can learn to type without looking at the keyboard. They can use this skill in the preparation of reports, cutting stencils for a class newspaper and numerous other activities.

35. Boys and girls may make rules for pupil behavior, pupil dress, safety and so on.

36. Bright pupils have studied optional units in order to explore new areas or to acquire information about people or places of interest.

Purposes of an Enrichment Program

Enrichment activities must have meaning and value; it does not mean more of the same. Enrichment really means giving students something more, something in addition to the normal curricular offering. Frequently educators refer to horizontal development of the curriculum as opposed to vertical development. The latter definition is more likely to be thought of in terms of acceleration, so it is not appropriate to use it to describe enrichment offerings. Teachers who are concerned with teaching prescribed content and skills tend to think of a vertical growth pattern and hold back for fear of encroaching on the domain of the next teacher. This may result in needless review and a minimum of meaningful experiences for the students. However, this need not be the case since numerous topics or problem areas can be studied if teachers elect to expand the curriculum.

Natural pupil curiosity is a powerful incentive but it is not exploited as much as it should be. What some teachers may consider extras should become part of the regular curriculum and should help meet basic pupil needs and satisfy as well as stimulate their curiosity and interests. When the program is developed horizontally the children can engage in activities that have meaning and value to the learner without being mere drill or busy-work. The learning activities should help in broadening the children's backgrounds and in their mastering of new skills. They should help pupils solve problems in terms of their experiences and stage of development. This means that many enrichment activities must be considered in terms of *individual* or *small-group* needs. If a pupil has a good background in one field the new activities should foster the development of competency in other fields of endeavor.

Unfortunately some teachers think of enrichment activities as rewards for accomplishment. As a result many average and below-average children may never have time to take part in good, stimulating, enriching activities. This does not happen in a good program. The slow-progressing pupil does not feel rejected or unwanted because the teacher sees to it that he takes part in some of the activities children are apt to think of as fun because they are a break from normal routines. In such classes the gifted pupils work at more advanced levels than the less capable pupils. If children are ready to engage in an enrichment activity they should do so, but this does not mean that enrichment activities are synonymous with fun. Many of them involve hard work. An immature pupil may find that his involvement in some of the extras can result in frustration unless he is highly interested in a project or sees values in it that are missing from the regular class activities.

Because gifted children can complete normal class requirements in less time than other pupils they will often have more time to devote to enrichment activities; however, some time should be made available to average and less-than-average children so that they can take part in activities based on some recognition of their own interests. Each pupil should be able to work in a rich program of activities. No child should feel slighted because pupils in the top group, instead of having to continue working in the "old arithmetic book," are allowed to read a play, go to the library or make up their own arithmetic examples. The enrichment program recognizes proficiency in basic skill areas and then aims at involving pupils in activities that help develop creativity. Gifted children when encouraged or motivated, will read beyond the textbook for greater appreciation, reflection and critical judgment. They will read both classic and modern literature. With guidance they will read whole books as well as short stories if they read in a program that has breadth and depth.

The teacher can provide children with enrichment activities in most subjects; however, she should have a clear picture in her own mind of the values or purposes underlying the activities. She should be able to justify her own activities and those of the boys and girls in terms of the broad objectives of the school and the needs of the children. The enrichment activities should help children realize both short-term and long-term objectives in the light of their abilities or stages of maturity. The teacher can teach without doing much to enrich the program but this type of teaching is meaningless for many children who need to go beyond a minimum program. Enrichment activities are based upon realizing some of the following types of objectives or goals:

1. *Enrichment activities are a means to an end, namely, the development of pupil abilities and skills to the maximum of the individual's potential.* Through enrichment activities the teacher expects to stimulate the individual to engage in activities that will help him to know himself, to know his strengths and weaknesses. The teacher strives to introduce the pupil to new resources that will enable him to solve problems within the realm of possibility if he will make the effort and take the time to solve them. The teacher does not want the learner to waste his potential for leadership or creativity. If he has talents, she wants him to discover them and then use them to satisfy his own needs for self-expression as well as to make a meaningful contribution to society.

2. *Enrichment activities help broaden the pupil's background of knowledge.* By going beyond the single textbook, the pupil is exposed to new sources of knowledge that should help him to acquire a broader background of knowledge. He should accumulate a wide background of knowledge in various subject fields based upon his readiness and need for this information. He reads widely in new fields and reads deeply in old ones. As he acquires a rich background of information he is able to make better choices and is able to see new problems to solve or new worlds to conquer.

3. *Enrichment activities help pupils develop a command of the fundamental skills.* The pupil should not be content to learn just the minimum. He is encouraged to master the fundamental processes and then become pro-

ficient in using them. In arithmetic he learns to apply the facts and skills he has learned, to solve problems on high intellectual levels. In the area of language arts he learns to express himself both orally and in writing. When he reads, he shows that he can read critically and with a very high degree of comprehension. In the field of social studies he shows that he has a background of information to deal effectively with personal, school, community or social problems. He has acquired the ability to locate information and do some type of research on an independent level. At the same time he has the ability to work as a member of a team whether on the playfield or in the classroom. In order to develop these skills the pupil has to have many rich experiences involving work with many mediums and with many types of people. These are essential if he is going to work at high levels in basic skill areas.

4. *Enrichment activities should lead to higher levels of understanding.* With enough application most boys and girls can memorize facts that may make them look good in the eyes of some teachers or parents but they have no actual value unless they are understood and can be applied. Children tend to take part in activities that will allow them to practice skills or apply knowledge. These experiences make up the enrichment part of many good programs. Through enrichment the pupil is encouraged to use the information he acquires in various subject fields, to reach higher levels of understanding and readiness for more difficult or advanced stages of learning.

5. *Enrichment activities should make the pupil want to reach new heights of learning.* Education should not be a passive process. The curriculum should be filled with activities that excite the pupil to the point that he wants to learn. When the teacher asks pupils to turn to their history books, there should not be a low groan from the students. The subject should be interesting and appealing to the pupils. At times the teacher can capitalize on the natural desires, interests or curiosities of the students. When this is not possible the teacher should be able to

stimulate interest in some aspects of the curriculum. In many instances this can be done through the introduction of some types of enrichment activities that will help pupils see a purpose in studying.

6. *Enrichment activities should help foster a desire for knowledge.* The ability to read is basic for pupil growth but mere ability to read at a high level is not sufficient for success in college or the world of business. Unless the pupil can find joy and satisfaction in intellectual pursuits he is unlikely to use his skill except under pressure. By the time boys and girls enter high school they should be reading widely because they want to read and not because a teacher tells them to do so. One does not reach this stage without long years of preparation based on many rich experiences that broaden children's backgrounds and help foster a further desire for knowledge.

7. *Enrichment activities should encourage the development of creativity.* Through working with many mediums and through wide exploration, the learner has a chance to discover whether or not he has any special talent. If the teacher finds a pupil has the ability to create, he should be encouraged to develop his talents. In many instances the pupil will find that enrichment activities are the ones that allow him to experiment and find himself. They may help him express himself through writing, drawing, speaking, painting, playing a musical instrument or experimenting with a phase of science. Each teacher has a responsibility to sponsor enrichment activities that will enable pupils to work in mediums that belong to the creative arts. Creative children cannot develop or blossom forth unless they have creative experiences, but in many instances they have to go through a readiness stage leading to creative expression just as much as they do for subjects such as reading and arithmetic.

8. *Enrichment activities should encourage pupil exploration of the environment.* The classroom should foster an atmosphere that is conducive to exploration and research. Enrichment activities should open up new worlds

to all students but particularly to pupils who have the ability to achieve at beyond-average expectancy levels. Each one may have to work hard to find success, but this should be compensated by the satisfactions that come from exploring new fields and getting better acquainted with the vast world beyond the normal range of expectation for a particular grade level or in a particular subject field.

The Dependency of Small Schools upon Enrichment

The number of truly gifted children in the classes of an average school tend to be small. Since many of these schools are not a part of a city school system, it may be difficult for the administrators to bring together enough gifted pupils to warrant the formation of special classes or to bring in specialists who can work with them on special projects or enrichment courses. In many instances the small schools will be able to meet the challenge through an ungraded program or through multiclass or multigrade groupings but in many other schools the classroom teachers will have to work alone with their problem children, be they bright or slow learners. It is in these small schools, for the most part, that teachers will have to depend upon enrichment to meet the challenge of educating their gifted pupils.

Following is a typical example of how the fast learner is often handled in the regular classroom.

In a general assignment for a class the teacher may find that average students may take a full forty minutes to do the required reading and answer her questions. Slow readers or slow-learning pupils may never complete the assignment unless they have additional time. When bright or fast learners face such an assignment, a special problem develops. They may be interested in the activity, but the fact that they read rapidly, digest the material easily and organize their thoughts with a minimum of rereading or pondering leaves them with a time problem. These pupils may easily finish the assignment in twenty to twenty-five minutes if not sooner. What should they do? They may have fifteen to twenty minutes to kill. In many such instances the teacher may merely say, "You may take out a book to read if you have finished." Up to a point this may be satisfying but unguided reading is not always enriching. One bright fifth grader was able to read five library books a week while waiting for others to catch up. This frustrated the teacher, so he ordered her to stop reading but did not give her anything else to do; as a result she finished the year in the class with her hands folded while her thoughts wandered far afield. Another solution some teachers have turned to involved the assignment of extra questions or extra examples that served no other purpose than to keep the fast learner from having too much free time on his hands. After a time some bright pupils realize what is happening. They know that the completion of an assignment ahead of time will only bring on more busy-work so they begin to pace their own progress in terms of average pupils. This slowdown eliminates the need for busy-work assignments but results in a pattern of poor work habits for the student which, over a number of years, can be disastrous. Many gifted pupils have learned how to kill time gracefully but others may become careless, with the result that their work is done in a slovenly manner because pride of accomplishment is gone. One teacher who had only one gifted pupil in her class was so frustrated with his speed of accomplishment that she invented errands to get him out of the way as much of the time as possible.

Other teachers have found that many of their problems with gifted pupils partially disappear when they can bring together pupils with special interests or abilities for special studies on an enrichment basis. Here small group activities centering about a series of optional units or advanced unit studies have eliminated the problem of keeping bright pupils busy. In other instances, where there are insufficient pupils on a common learning level to form a teachable group, the development of pupil specialties has been helpful.

Boys and girls who have grown up in a school where all their teachers have arranged for them to take part in enrichment and supplementary activities will not be overly concerned when a teacher gives them an assignment that will require extra work or effort. They have become accustomed to working in depth. They know the meaning of responsibility, so if the teacher helps them see the value of such an activity, they find no need to question further. The problem arises when boys and girls who have not been trained to accept new or additional responsibilities are faced with extra work; a problem also arises when they do not understand the meaning of enrichment activities. Having had little experience with broadening activities, these pupils may look at the special project as a challenge to their liberty. However, young children who have found satisfaction and success in their school work will accept the enrichment activities as part of the daily program—even if some must expend extra effort. Furthermore, boys and girls can learn to work together without feeling jealous even if some students are engaging in activities that appear to be fun while others are still trying to master fundamentals. Here training and experience from an early age are an asset for pupil acceptance and cooperation in a program where the special needs of gifted pupils are met by enrichment.

The teacher in a small school may have to move slowly when introducing enrichment experiences to pupils who have had few such experiences. She may have to set the stage for a new pattern of work and a new attitude towards work. This may be done by involving pupils in preliminary stages through discussion and pupil-teacher planning. If the teacher plans a unit with the students, she can guide them to take assignments that appeal to their interests. Natural leadership should be encouraged, but at the same time the teacher can take steps that will help place potential leaders in positions where they can develop into leaders. At times the teacher will have to forego pushing some students because the class or group is not ready to recognize their leadership qualities. Untrained or inexperienced children may want to give leadership responsibilities to the most popular pupil instead of the most qualified individual. If this is so they may have to experience some failures and frustrations as a result of following poor leaders. Sometimes the teacher can resolve this problem by rotating chairmanships so that other pupils will have a chance to assume a leadership role. In time the students will be able to look for leaders who have the qualities of leadership. Sometimes these become evident in an evaluation period where the boys and girls discover or are shown how time and energy were wasted because of poor leadership.

Children who have opportunities to work on committees or special projects soon learn to accept the pupil who has to spend extra time in the library on a research problem. It helps when pupils can volunteer for projects of their own choice but the teacher may have to guide students toward continuing to work with materials that are challenging and within their range of ability or understanding. The teacher may also have to talk with the pupils to discover their interests or to help them acquire new interests.

There will be times when children engage in activities that they may not enjoy, but if the teacher has a good supply of reference materials and teaching aids, pupil curiosity will often motivate them to engage in activities where they will find new interests. Many enrichment activities may not involve unit activity, but the teacher in the small school will often find that she can do a great deal more for pupils at either end of the intellectual scale by choosing enrichment activities of a unit nature.

Enrichment Leads to Acceleration

Enrichment activities must promote growth. However, the growth must be at a steady rather than a rapid pace. The teacher should emphasize quality education through depth learning rather than hasty and narrow approaches to learning. With such an approach the pupil is not concerned with how many pages of arithmetic he can complete as much as how well he knows what he has done. The aim is not to finish learning how to spell a given list of words in half the given time; the essential point is that the pupil has the opportunity to use the words so that they become a part of his oral or written vocabulary. Enrichment is one approach to the problem of application. Through involvement in many types of enrichment activities the pupil can reach higher levels of accomplishment and understanding than are reached by pupils who continue to work day after day in the same basic textbook in the same old way.

7 Meeting Needs Through Special Programs and Activities

Numerous school systems are trying to meet the needs of gifted boys and girls through some form of acceleration or enrichment. While the concept of the special class continues to have support from educators and parents there are some schools that attempt to provide for their gifted students in the regular classroom. In other communities special programs and activities both in the classroom and beyond the confines of the school are offered in an attempt to motivate gifted students and broaden their backgrounds to the point where they will make a special effort to excel in one or more fields of study. This chapter will deal with some of the ways a community can more effectively provide for the needs of its gifted students.

Subgrouping Activities in the Regular Classroom

Primary grade teachers generally have a better understanding of what is meant by subgrouping than upper grade teachers. The latter think of grouping in terms of homogeneous grouping on the basis of class or divisions within a school. This is in contrast to the formation of a heterogeneous class broken into small learning groups for reading, arithmetic and spelling activities. Pupil success in a given field of study here becomes the basis for the instruction provided by the teacher and by the books used by the pupils. Bright pupils are most often found in the top reading or arithmetic groups although differences in interests and backgrounds are such that pupils in the top section in one class may not be in a comparable group for another subject area of study.

If the teachers are flexible and have adequate materials it is possible to accelerate the curriculum for gifted pupils in the regular classroom. Thus, a group of bright pupils may finish normal grade requirements in the space of six or seven months. The teacher may then concentrate on a general broadening of pupil backgrounds for a time, but if they are ready for higher-level learning activities she must be free to promote them without fear that she is encroaching on the domain of higher-level teachers. If teachers accept pupils as they are, the gifted pupils need not be frustrated in the normal classroom. The principles of subgrouping can be used at all grade levels and in all subject fields, including chemistry and physics, English and social studies. Unfortunately, many teachers do not understand the role they should play in working with their bright pupils and thereby make more work for themselves than is necessary. For example, many teachers are so addicted to the concept of meeting classes every day that they are reluctant to accept a program that may call for a meeting with gifted pupils only three times a week. Slow learners and average learners need to work much more closely with their teachers than bright pupils both because they are not as ready to work independently and because they need more concrete experiences before moving into new learning activities. In contrast many gifted pupils are able to work out directions or procedures with a minimum of teacher help. If they have problems, other gifted pupils are able to help them locate their source of trouble.

Balanced or Cluster Groupings in Small Group Activities

When pupils are assigned to a classroom with the aim of maintaining a heterogeneous class section, the range of pupil needs and accomplishments may prevent the teacher from achieving desired goals. Her task can be simplified without sacrificing the concept of heterogeneous sectioning by balanced grouping. This means that the school administrator and his teachers deliberately balance out the top or bottom sections to insure that sufficient bright or slow-learning pupils will be assigned to the teacher to form teachable subgroups within the class. As an example, it is not fair to each of five teachers to have one or two bright pupils and one or two slow learners in a class that has a broad range of average learners. The needs of both classifications of students will be met much more effectively if five or six bright pupils can be assigned to one teacher and a similar number of the slowest learning pupils to another. Each teacher is automatically guaranteed sufficient numbers of pupils with common needs or at a common learning point to justify the formation of a learning or work group. When a single bright pupil is assigned to a class he neither gets the teacher's attention nor the competition he needs. However, if at least five, six or seven pupils have reached the same stage of intellectual development or achievement level, the teacher is able to plan specific activities for and with them.

Each classroom teacher can thus have a cluster of pupils who need her time and attention without feeling that she has to ignore pupils in another learning category. In view of large class enrollments the goal should be to limit the number of subgroups within a class to a maximum of three. This is quite possible at the primary grade level, but because of the achievement spread at upper grade levels balanced grouping may necessitate a greater homogeneity in the fifth, sixth and seventh grades than is commonly accepted by those advocating heterogeneous grouping. Intermediate grade and upper grade teachers may find balanced grouping will be most effective if some form of cross-grade grouping is accepted. In the smaller schools this will allow teachers to work with small clusters or groups of students who have common needs. Gifted pupils in the school where balanced grouping is recognized will find themselves working with peermates who have reached a common learning level. If the other students lack extremely high intellectual skill, the gifted pupil may soon outdistance many of his classmates, but this barrier can be overcome through some individualization of the pupil schedule and the establishment of transfer points if the range of accomplishment in a given classroom becomes too great to enable the teacher to work smoothly and efficiently.

Multiple Texts and Mixed Sets in Regular Classrooms

Many teachers who may not be up to teaching in a subgrouping approach may achieve desired goals by use of multiple texts or mixed sets. The teacher can provide a new challenge to all pupils in her classroom without actually divorcing herself from a mass teaching technique. She will have to modify the way she makes assignments and may have to accept the fact that some pupils will reach higher level goals than others when working with material by different authors.

1. *Teaching with multiple texts.* The teacher orders several textbooks for a subject from different publishers. Some of them may be easier than others or may even deal with special phases of a subject. Pupils are expected to find answers to problems through reading and study in books they can understand. Page-by-page assignments are eliminated when students learn to use the index and table of contents to find references to broad topics that engage

the attention of the entire class. Thus, a very slow learner or a pupil who reads at a low level may refer to a book that treats the Civil War very lightly or in general terms, in contrast with the gifted pupil, who is directed to find specific references to more complex phases of the Civil War. The gifted pupil will be expected to develop an awareness of the fundamental reasons for the great conflict, some of the problems of the North in obtaining a winning team of generals and an understanding of the problems of reconstruction that may hardly be mentioned in the simpler reference books.

Teaching with multiple textbooks may make teaching more complex for the teacher since she is no longer able to read from a single textbook with the expectation that all members of the class will be able to follow the reader as he goes from word to word or from line to line. Teachers who have learned to use the multiple text technique find their work is more stimulating to themselves as well as to their students. This is especially true where the pupils report that different writers have emphasized a different point or have even contradicted one another. The use of multiple texts may help gifted pupils work up specialties. Here the teacher anticipates a special theme or area of study and motivates the gifted pupil to begin studying ahead of time in order to make a special report or become a resource person for others when the entire class begins to study the new theme or unit.

2. *Teaching with mixed sets.* A given class may work with two or three different textbooks instead of a basic textbook. In the former category a class may have had reference to two or three books by an author, but in the mixed-set approach the teacher may have planned on a minimum of twelve or fifteen copies of each of two or three basic textbooks. This enables her to work with pupils on a subgrouping basis if she is not satisfied with what they do as individuals. In selecting the two or three titles that will comprise a mixed set of textbooks the teacher will often try to obtain books that provide differ-

ent treatments of the subject or that are written on different learning levels. In one case vocabulary and sentence structure may be a criterion; in another case the criterion may be illustrations; and in the third case the critical element may be the depth or detail.

In either the multiple text or the mixed-set approach gifted pupils are given a chance to assume leadership roles and at the same time the mediocrity necessary for the preservation of the heterogeneity concept is not sacrificed. They can continue to work within the framework of a common theme but their studies can take them into a broad study of some phases of a topic. With clear-cut marking standards the gifted pupils have to produce on a high level if they expect to receive marks based on high levels of achievement and good work-study patterns.

Homogeneous Grouping

Many educators favor homogeneous over heterogeneous grouping as a more effective program for meeting the needs of gifted pupils. In theory, homogeneous grouping can bring together students who have common educational needs although the evidence has not been readily obtainable to support the claim that pupils assigned to homogeneous sections of a classroom attain higher learning levels than those left in heterogeneous class groupings. In a sense the special class for the gifted is an extreme form of homogeneous grouping in that pupils with a common background of ability are separated from those lacking in outstanding talents or intellectual ability. In most secondary schools the top level sections of a class may include some intellectually gifted students, but they may be in a minority.

Homogeneous classes may be formed around a number of common elements such as intelligence, reading achievement, interests and general recommendations of teachers based upon report card grades or subjective teacher

opinions. Unfortunately, many of the teachers of a homogeneously formed class fail to accept the fact that wide
differences in achievement, interest, motivation and ability can still be found in their classrooms. If there is a
common base at the beginning of the year, the differences
may begin to appear within a few weeks as the faster
learners begin to accelerate their mastery of fundamental
processes and the accumulation of essential background
material. In such classes the attempt to use a mass approach to teaching can become as deadening and frustrating an experience for gifted pupils as mass teaching is for
pupils assigned to classes heterogeneously. If pupils are to
work most effectively in homogeneously formed classes
they must still be exposed to subgrouping techniques or to
a program that recognizes individuality when it comes to
learning. One of the reasons homogeneous groups have
not attained desired goals may be the failure to provide a
different curriculum and different evaluative procedures
to those working in the high and low groups. For instance, gifted pupils who are assigned to a top-level history class may not gain very much if they study the same
basic textbooks as pupils in lower-level class sections. The
problem is compounded when everyone takes the same
final examination. If the system is to be truly effective
some form of tracking may be necessary. This means that
pupils will move through a school or series of grades on
the basis of a curriculum that has been modified in terms
of different ability or interest levels. Thus gifted pupils
who are assigned to a top-level or fast-learning group will
be expected to cover more ground and work in greater
depth than pupils assigned to a lower-level track.

Honors Classes

In an attempt to provide a challenging program for gifted
pupils, a large number of high schools have formed what
they call Honor classes in English, mathematics, science

or social studies. Pupils assigned to Honor classes may have to maintain a special standard of performance if they are to remain in a program developed to challenge their special abilities or interests. Thus, a pupil in an advanced Honors French class or English class may be expected to obtain no mark lower than 85 if he is to *remain* with his class. This calls for the continuation of high-level performance on the part of many gifted pupils. However, some gifted pupils have elected to drop back to an ordinary section of the college-bound curriculum in order to escape the pressure or to work at what could be considered a more restful pace since they can continue to obtain high marks with a minimum of effort. (This occurs where no attempt is made to differentiate between marks obtained in an Honors course and in a non-Honors course.)

One high school has developed an Honors school within the regular high school. Pupils are grouped together who have selected special programs. For example, all pre-engineering students follow a course of study designed to meet their special needs. Placement in such courses is based upon IQ, reading achievement, arithmetic achievement and teacher ratings; however, pupils who fail to come up to expected achievement standards may be re-tested before being assigned to regular classes. Pupils in the Honors school join the rest of the student body for nonacademic activities.

The Honors class may lead to advanced placement but it may mean merely that the pupils have completed programs of study that called for special achievement and high accomplishment. In some schools pupils in the Honors class may be given special privileges such as freedom to work without having to meet regular homeroom or study hall requirements. In one school they are given free access to special laboratories or reference work centers. In other schools they are automatically given permission to manage their free time in order to complete special projects or research assignments, to read in the library, to type papers or to confer with teachers.

Advanced Placement

Educators are not in complete accord regarding the value of the Advanced Placement Program; however, the popularity of such programs has continued since the inception of the plan back in the early 1950's.

1. *The Early Admissions Program.* This program opened the doors to a new type of acceleration. It started in 1951 when a group of twelve colleges and universities admitted as college freshmen a number of students who had completed only their sophomore or junior year of high school and who were, as a result, a year or two younger than the average entering freshmen.

Most of the students who were admitted to college early could be described as falling into the gifted category although a number of them were classified as having only average ability. Paschal's study showed that academically, these special students outperformed both their classmates and the comparison group of equally capable but older students who had completed high school. In social and economic adjustment they were equal to the comparison group and to their other classmates. In many instances the early admissions students assumed leadership roles and exhibited a maturity far beyond what might have been expected of them.

Most frequently cited as advantages were the greater academic challenges of college work compared with what students would have been doing had they remained in high school for the last two years and the opportunity to enter professional study, a career or marriage earlier. On the basis of the evidence it is apparent that carefully selected students who are given the opportunity to move into college early will not be injured by that experience either academically or socially.

2. *The Advanced Placement Program.* Shortly after the start of the Early Admissions Program seven schools served as pioneers for what has since become known as the Advanced Placement Program. In 1954 a report,

"College Admission With Advanced Standing," was given in which the participating colleges agreed that students who completed the work described in a satisfactory manner, as tested on examinations, would be given advanced college placement credit. Following this report the College Entrance Examination Board began to construct and administer special examinations to provide colleges and schools with grades and other data on the credit and standing of pupils who had taken advanced placement tests.

Recent studies of high school students who were able to bypass traditional freshman courses because of their advanced standing have shown that they can work successfully in the higher level courses. Their achievement compares favorably with college students who took a full sequence of courses in the regular college setting. As a rule students in the Advanced Placement Program are seldom accelerated as much as a year although Harvard has had some entering students who came with the equivalent of two years advanced preparation. The usual limited acceleration may be attributed to the failure of the high school to offer enough advanced courses to warrant a student taking more than one or two of the Advanced Placement Examinations.

Ducanis' study of Advanced Placement in New York State shows that only 28 per cent of the high schools in the State were participating in the program; however, more than 5700 New York State students from 330 high schools took Advanced Placement Examinations in the May, 1963 testing session. Most of the students took the examinations for English, mathematics or American history although students have also taken examinations in biology, chemistry, foreign languages (French, German, Latin, Spanish), European history and French literature.

For the most part students who take Advanced Placement examinations come from Honors courses or special Advanced Placement Programs offered in their respective high schools or in a nearby college. Not every pupil who takes the special examination achieves the goal of entering college with advanced standing. In some instances the fault may lie with the student but in other cases the pupil's failure to gain recognition for extra effort may be attributed to a faulty high school curriculum, poorly prepared teachers or the lack of adequate teaching materials. For example, many students make a poor showing on the English Composition Test, thus pointing up the need to review earlier English standards or teaching procedures.

The Advanced Placement Program is considered by the authors to be one solution to the problem of acceleration for intellectually gifted students. They would, however, broaden the concept of advanced placement to make it possible for all exceptionally talented students to take advanced placement examinations in any area or field of study where they feel especially competent regardless of whether the prospective student had taken part in an Honors program or an approved Advanced Placement Program. The examination would be considered evidence that the pupil had developed sufficient proficiency to work in advanced level courses since many gifted pupils are capable of accelerating into higher-level learning activities on the basis of their own self-improvement programs or special interests.

Acceptance of Gifted High School Students as Part-time College Students

A small number of colleges arrange for bright high school students to take regular Freshmen courses before they graduate. Juniors may take college-level courses during the summer while Seniors may take college courses during the winter session. If the students meet the college requirements for a given course they are given regular college credit for it, thereby making it possible for the pupils to enter college with advanced standing. If the students elect to take a college course while they are still in high school, they are excused from a parallel high school course. Generally, the prerequisite for such courses is an IQ of 125 or higher plus high achievement scores on standardized achievement tests and/or on College Board Examinations. A positive recommendation from the high school staff or guidance counselor is essential.

One college accepts talented music students during the summer following the Junior year. The recommended students may take up to eight hours of music courses in a six-week summer session. Another college will place recommended high school students in Freshmen courses in mathematics, English, world history, chemistry, French, German, Spanish and biology. These students work beside regular college students during the regular school year, but in the summer period an entire class may consist of bright or gifted students. These students may take one full course in an eight-week summer session taught by regular college professors in college classrooms.

Special Enrichment Programs
in High Schools

While a number of high schools definitely label some courses advanced or accelerated courses, a few schools elect to limit their programs to courses labeled enrichment courses. They may merely include more filler material that serves no practical purpose or they may include enough new and challenging material so that students cannot help but enjoy learning activities that were previously vague and meaningless because the teacher was trying to get through a textbook or course of study. An outsider may have to study a program carefully to appreciate what new elements have been added to the curriculum.

Unfortunately, many educators continue to interpret the word *enrichment* differently. In one school it refers to the rapid acceleration of pupils through a mathematics program so that the students can begin algebra one year earlier. In another school the pupils complete Latin I and Latin II in one and one-half years so that the pupils can begin readings normally assigned to later years. In a third school the pupils rush through seventh and eighth grade science and overlap into ninth grade science in order to begin biology in the ninth grade.

The question may well be raised whether enrichment should consist of vertical or horizontal growth. In the foregoing illustrations the acceleration into advanced-level courses may be questioned in terms of the true meaning of enrichment. Can one feel certain that the acceleration of pupils through a designated curriculum carried with it understanding and appreciation of the subject? If so, vertical growth may be considered desirable for gifted and nongifted alike; however, it seems much more practical to use some of the extra time for a wide horizontal expansion of the curriculum to ensure that the students understand the materials and ideas introduced in the regular program. One definition of the word *enrichment* calls for activities that enable boys and girls to explore their interests and to have time to study an area in depth while finding a variety of ways to express themselves creatively. Vertical growth will still be possible in such a situation, but in this approach the individual may reach these higher levels with a much more complete understanding of the forces that make the world tick.

One ninth grade class read every page of a Civics text. The students were quizzed and tested until they were considered ready to begin a new course. On the surface they had achieved a series of goals when they passed the tests but the question could be asked whether they had actually reached the point where they understood the role they would ultimately play as adult citizens. In contrast, the pupils in a second Civics class used their text as a guide but did not always struggle with all the definitions and complex phraseology. One week the class visited the State Library where they saw their State Constitution. A visit to the State prison was made several weeks after sitting in on a court session. A speaker from the Department of Conservation told them what their government was doing to prevent erosion. Over the course of the year these pupils talked with government officials and saw a number of films that dealt with topics of common interest.

When a final test was given to the pupils in the two different classes, the pupils in the second section obtained much higher scores although the ability of the two groups was comparable. Many educators attribute the superior achievement to the provision of a variety of experiences that gave meaning to a curriculum.

The Unit Approach

The unit approach is considered essential to the fullest development of the talents and educational potential of gifted students. Students assigned to a special class for gifted children can follow the unit approach most effectively; however, some high schools tend to emphasize traditional approaches to the neglect of experiences more often associated with a unitary approach. This is evident in the concentration on the mastery of subject matter through rote learning based on the use of a single textbook or a lecture/question-and-answer approach. The unit can become the medium through which gifted children either in a regular classroom or in a special class can learn the meaning of democratic processes. In addition it gives them many opportunities to explore their interests, to develop leadership qualities and to demonstrate creative talents. The unit gives them many opportunities to work through individualized assignments in areas of special interest or in areas where special abilities can be extended. Thus, an interest in art may be utilized to dramatize the Mendelian theory pictorially. Original stories can be written by students at all grade levels to show understanding and appreciation of a topic or theme. Groups of students may cooperate in the writing of a play or the dramatization of one.

Basic to the development of a unit is competence in research skills. While these essential skills can be taught at lower grade levels, the real opportunity to master them should come in the fifth, sixth, seventh and eighth grade classes. Gifted students, especially, should master them through many opportunities to work independently and collectively in their search for knowledge and new skills. How successfully these students achieve the desired goals can be evaluated in their special papers for high school and college teachers. Unfortunately many bright students do not learn until it is too late that their good memories will not suffice when they are asked to complete a research paper for a college course. In many instances this is their first experience with this type of assignment. Such mishaps do not have to occur if boys and girls learn how to seek information from the many mediums of expression while at lower elementary and secondary school levels.

Pursuit of Special Interests Through a Released-time Program

A number of schools allow selected students to pursue their own interests by releasing them from school early or by excusing them for special activities. The students often use this extra time to attend special seminars or to engage in research activities.

One group of students may set up experiments in science during periods when they are released from regular classrooms. They are given access to laboratories and special equipment necessary for the completion of their projects. They may consult with teachers and give special reports or demonstrations to other students.

Students in one high school meet for a special class in creative writing. At times they work with a teacher but each student selects the type of writing he prefers and then spends hours developing a plot or theme. From time to time the students meet to read to the class what they have written and to discuss their problems.

Selected students attend weekly seminars devoted to the study of great books. The pupils read from a selected bibliography in preparation for lectures by faculty members and authorities from nearby colleges or the community itself. The students discuss what they have read or heard with each other and with the lecturers.

Enrichment in Hobby Clubs

From an early age gifted students use their curiosity and wide interests to develop special hobbies. The school staff can encourage gifted students in the development of their hobbies and in the discovery of new interests. In many schools enrichment is provided for gifted students through hobby clubs that meet during a school activity period or after school. In the elementary school a club may be interested in rocks, stamps, birds, music or art, while at the high school level the special clubs may promote interest in biology, physics, mathematics, French, Latin, debating skill, dancing, writing and other areas that allow pupils to broaden their backgrounds and to acquire experiences not acquired in the regular classroom.

Introduction of Foreign Languages in Primary Grades

Boys and girls who show ability in the primary grades are introduced to the study of a foreign language. In some schools a second language may be started with fourth or fifth graders but others commence instruction at the second and third grade level. A few schools have even exposed the first graders to a foreign language with the expectation that they will continue the study of the language through elementary and junior high schools and with the understanding that they will be placed in advanced foreign language classes when they reach high school. While French and Spanish are favored, elementary school students have also studied Italian, German and Russian. In some schools the regular teacher may introduce the new language to the pupils; in other schools a special teacher may be employed to teach the children. She may be a teacher borrowed from the high school staff, or she may be a full-time foreign language teacher trained to work with younger children. In one elementary school Russian was taught to selected second grade pupils by a parent who was most proficient in the language and in working with young children.

Foreign languages have been taught through the use of records and specially prepared tapes. Teachers who lacked proficiency in a new language have been aided by experts who used television to communicate with interested students. At the primary grade level children acquire a foreign language vocabulary through an audiolingual approach. If they show skill in speaking, they are introduced to reading and writing the language when they reach the intermediate grades.

Community Programs

Special classes are frequently offered outside the school to talented and gifted students. Many of these classes are held on Saturday mornings; others may be held after school. Pupils may join a class in the library to read and talk about good books. Others may go to a museum to study art or to draw and paint. Still others may meet in special halls where they can learn to dance, weave, sculpt or develop dramatic talents. Some pupils join choral or instrumental groups while others follow science interests.

Many communities have organizations that will readily support a class for gifted children. Some will provide financial aid, but more important than money is the leadership they can give to pupils who will give up their free time to work with adults who have some special skill or interest. In one school system the Parent Teacher Association located talented men and women in the community who could provide leadership at Saturday morning classes on a voluntary basis. In another school system the parents raised money to employ talented individuals to teach dramatics, sculpturing and dancing.

In a number of communities the public supports special summer camps or workshops for selected students. Those who attend these camps may study new subjects or increase skill in areas where they need extra help or have special interest. The workshops may stress academic growth but many of them encourage the growth of creative skill.

Obtaining the services of volunteers for classes that meet regularly on Saturdays or during the summer is not always easy, but those who would like to bring new life into their classes will often find that they are surrounded by resource people who have a special skill or talent they would occasionally like to share. All it takes is an invitation and some encouragement to get these individuals before a group of children. Individual boys and girls can leave their classrooms to interview leading citizens in their community, but there are many men and women willing to bring a wealth of experience and ideas to a class.

In one community the Women's Club compiled a small booklet containing the names of resource people in the community who would serve as consultants to teachers and students interested in their hobbies or field of work. Each new teacher received a copy of the booklet and if the teacher was new to the community someone was assigned to serve as a contact agent.

Special Help Programs for Disadvantaged Children

Educators who work with boys and girls from low social and economic areas frequently have difficulty when they try to establish special programs for potentially gifted children. One of their first barriers is that of identifying individuals who can profit from a special program; however, Non-Verbal Group IQ tests plus individual IQ tests help screen out prospective candidates for special help programs. Pupils rated in the top achieving section of their classes or thought gifted in a creative subject such as art and music may be considered outstanding even though general achievement does not exceed or even reach normal grade level standards. The selection of those pupils falling into the top 10 per cent of the academic students and the top 10 per cent of the potentially talented (that is, in music, art, dance, mechanical aptitude, social leadership, dramatics or creative writing) can be considered a step in the direction of a positive program to conserve both intellectual and nonintellectual talent in culturally disadvantaged children.

Studies have shown that some resistance may be encountered from students and parents in special help programs; therefore a social worker can be a most valuable member of the staff since she can enter homes and help parents understand the value of a higher horizon type of program. Two other important staff members are the school psychologist and the guidance counselor. The first can give diagnostic and consultant help to teachers, and the second can help pupils try to find solutions to personal and vocational problems.

While all disadvantaged children benefit from special attention, it is essential that those who fall into the high underachiever category be given a forward boost or push. They need a program that allows them to acquire repeated tastes of success. This may require hand-tailoring of pupils' schedules instead of continued block-scheduling. They may have to be excused from some school activities in order to be free to participate in a broad program of enrichment activities. At times they will have to receive remedial instruction in subject areas where achievement exceeds one and a half to two years below expectation for their ability. If extra help is not available for all subjects, teachers may concentrate on the improvement of oral and written speech. Help in reading is essential, but pupils require good reading materials and a time and place to read for enjoyment as well as for knowledge. This may call for small class sectioning and individualized programing.

Special help programs are needed in rural as well as in urban areas. The children may be classified as poor Mexicans, Puerto Ricans, Chinese, Negroes or whites, but they will have one common bond, namely, a lack of motivation and understanding of the value of rich educational experiences. From this vast reservoir of deprived children can come the scientists, the authors, the poets, the musicians and the leaders of tomorrow if the school and other cooperating agencies can get through to them. Small classes and continued exposure to the finer things in life are just one phase in the special help program. The school may have to pay for extra cultural activities such as field trips to museums, plays and colleges; but there may have to be, in addition, provisions for a meaningful work experience to provide the young adolescents with pocket money and the feeling that they are capable of doing something worthwhile on their own. If these potentially talented pupils from disadvantaged homes can actually achieve personal success in other than academic areas they will be more susceptible to pleas from guidance counselors to continue their education when they are tempted to drop out of school. Pilot programs have shown the value of a released-time or school-work program in keeping potentially gifted pupils from becoming early dropouts.

An approach that has received little consideration so far but that can help many disadvantaged, gifted and non-gifted alike, achieve higher educational goals is that of the extended school year program. By providing an extra thirty days of continued instruction with good teachers in the first few years of schooling, there is a good chance that the acquisition of an extra year of enriching and broadening experiences will minimize the frustrations that often turn gifted boys and girls against higher-level educational opportunities. This extra time, plus the advantages of special help programs, can also eliminate some of the juvenile delinquency so common in low socioeconomic areas.

Help from Industries

Each summer some industries provide employment to a number of bright pupils. One large plant places promising science students in their laboratories where technicians and scientists talk with the students and help them master new skills. The students find their summers financially rewarding and in many instances acquire insight into a field of work that can lead to a career. Due to age restrictions some industries must limit their employment to college students; however, a few high school students are given employment and training in areas where there are no hazardous conditions.

In one community a leading pharmaceutical plant makes it a practice to solicit recommendations from the Director of Guidance. She provides the background on several of the most promising juniors and seniors. The students are interviewed if they are interested in summer employment, and those who pass the oral test are generally guaranteed a profitable and enlightened summer.

Many high school students need work experience before they go off to college, but they find work is not always available. If business and industry can find ways to give these bright pupils a chance to acquire a feeling of independence and an understanding of how the world outside the classroom operates, society as a whole will benefit. Bright and talented boys and girls often fail to pursue a college program because they have not learned what it means to work outside the classroom. A good work experience can play an important part in the direction they take.

Even a temporary job may restore a talented student's faith in himself. In some cases the fact that such students were able to earn enough money to purchase their own clothes, buy an old car or even support themselves for a short time gives them the satisfaction they need to return to their studies in the fall. For some young people social pressures plus an honest desire to do something useful are powerful motivating forces. While a good summer school program helps some of these boys and girls use up their energy and keeps them out of trouble, others really need the release that comes with a profitable work experience either in or out of school.

Recommendations for the Small School

The principal of a small elementary school or a small high school will, because of the small enrollment, always have problems if he tries to develop special classes for gifted pupils; therefore, a number of plans are recommended for consideration. While some of these have been mentioned previously we wish to group here, for convenience, a few recommendations of special pertinence to the small school.

1. *Separate classes for gifted pupils may be developed for pupils from several school districts.* It has been common practice in many school districts to share responsibility for the education of retarded pupils through cooperative action. The same principle can be extended to the gifted. For example, one school district could establish a special class for gifted intermediate grade pupils on a shared tuition basis. The students identified as potentially gifted pupils in a given school district would be transported to and from the school providing the classroom space, the teacher and the essential tools and equipment. A second school district may provide special classes for junior high school youngsters while a third school district may elect to make special provisions for talented pupils. All these endeavors may be developed cooperatively by local school administrators and teachers, or else the efforts may be guided by county or state educational

leaders who recognize the need for standards and who may be able to give guidance and encouragement to the teachers of the special classes.

2. *A county or regional school for gifted children can be developed.* Because of limited numbers of potentially gifted students in a given community the small school district cannot begin to emulate programs such as are found in the Cleveland Major Work Classes or in The Hunter College Elementary School in New York City. While the special shared class remains a possibility, the answer may lie in the establishment of special regional schools for gifted pupils. By combining resources, several communities may bring together enough gifted and specially talented students to warrant the establishment of a school with an entire staff oriented to the gifted child concept. In the large suburban areas close to our metropolitan districts the pupils can still be classified as commuters; but in the South and the Far West a type of boarding school could be established for those who would have to travel too far to warrant the establishment of special bus or taxi routes (although it may not be too unrealistic to think of a day when helicopters may be used to transport large numbers of pupils from cluster points to a distant educational center).

Current thinking is still limited to action by cooperative boards of education, but the important role now being assumed by the Federal Government in forming improved educational programs may make it possible to establish special schools for highly gifted (135 IQ and over) pupils. These schools can emphasize training in science, mathematics, art, music and electronics. With support from state and Federal sources, special equipment and a rich library can be brought to a central point for use by teachers and students alike. For example, closed circuit television can be used within the school to give depth to the program, and computers may not be out of the question for the study of pupil needs and the development of a master schedule to help meet these needs.

3. *Special classes may be taught through closed circuit*

television. School districts with limited enrollments can combine to bring in quality television programs via coaxial cables. The programs can originate in centers where highly qualified instructors can prepare the type of lessons that will appeal to gifted students. These teachers may be highly qualified elementary or high school teachers, or they may be members of a nearby college staff. Leading national figures from government or business may supplement the efforts of the regular staff. Inside the schools teachers may be employed to work with these gifted pupils, following guides prepared for the courses in advance—although a type of correspondence school arrangement may facilitate the evaluation of the work done by the teachers. New advances in the field of telephone communication can enhance the possibilities of contact being maintained by the television instructor whose students are located in schools many miles away from the studio. Thus, two, three or four students taking a course in analytical chemistry may speak to a distant instructor by means of group telephonic equipment.

4. *The gifted child specialists.* A gifted child specialist may be employed to work with teachers and pupils from several school districts. He may serve as a consultant to communities striving to develop independent programs for selected groups of children. In this case his work may be limited to helping the classroom teachers understand the nature of the gifted student and the way the curriculum should be modified to strengthen his program. Another approach may call for the use of a number of specialists to work directly with gifted and talented pupils on a rotation plan of school visitation. They may give lectures and/or demonstrations, direct student activities in areas of their specialty and guide the pupils in the use of new teaching machines for programed learning activities.

5. *The traveling library.* Many small schools lack the books that appeal to intellectually gifted students; therefore, the traveling library may be one answer to the problem of adequate reference materials. A start can

often be made with the county mobile library, but small school districts may find a special traveling high school library such as the one circulated by the American Association for the Advancement of Science with the support of the National Science Foundation. This traveling library provides the schools with selected books dealing with science, mathematics and good literature for at least one month. Teachers, librarians, and students who use the traveling library are able to supplement what is often a very limited and meager school or community library.

6. *The traveling classroom.* Special exhibits and equipment may be brought to small schools by means of trailers or special railroad cars. While the general nature of these traveling exhibits may be of interest to all students in the extremely small school, they fill a special need for bright pupils who require the stimulation of another world. To these intellectually starved students traveling cultural groups may bring personalities and subjects beyond the capability of any one school system working independently. Thus, a traveling band of musicians, actors, poets and writers provides a source of enrichment and challenge to boys and girls who would otherwise never come in contact with a culture other than the remote farming, lumbering or small industrial community.

7. *Teaching machines for gifted pupils.* Advanced classes may be too costly to establish in small communities, but this should not limit the exposure of gifted students to higher learning activities. The students can still work at advanced levels through a number of teaching machines. With teacher guidance they can pursue the study of subjects independently. For example, commercially prepared foreign language tapes may give the students the opportunity to master a rare foreign language or perhaps a fourth year of a language generally not offered for lack of enough students to warrant a section. The teaching machine can be used at all grade levels to individualize programs or to enrich a program for a group of interested students.

8. *The nongraded curriculum.* Few schools have developed what may be truly classified as a nongraded
curriculum although many elementary schools give lip
service to the term. If the small school will eliminate
traditional grade lines and concentrate on the teaching of
common skills and essential knowledge on the basis of
achievement instead of chronological age or grade, bright
children will be able to advance to higher learning levels
much more readily than they do when confined to a
graded curriculum. The establishment of nongraded
classes in the small high school can eliminate considerable
duplication of effort. For example, bright pupils can avoid
repetitious lessons on the parts of speech and sentence
construction if they can work with older students who
have a common need, namely, an interest in literature,
poetry or creative writing. Mastery of essential skills or
bodies of knowledge can be measured by special unit tests.
In many instances the gifted pupils join higher learning
groups through independent study and research activities
that provide background for the desired new activities.

In the small elementary school the duplication of
teacher effort may be eliminated through cross-grade
grouping. This makes it possible for pupils from several
traditional grade levels to meet and work in areas of
reading, arithmetic, science, social studies or language on
the basis of interest or level of accomplishment. While
this type of school organization may partially destroy the
old concept of the self-contained classroom, it has value in
that boys and girls can advance more readily into the
fields of endeavor that are necessarily limited in those
classrooms where the teacher is struggling to cope with
the equivalent of an achievement range extending through
several grades. (For example, the typical fifth grade
teacher is working with a range of at least five grade
levels of achievement. This range extends upward as
pupils move to higher grade levels.) Studies made of
pupils working in classrooms that include students from
several age or grade classifications show that many traditional objections to mixing grades disappear when the

pupils can see their own growth. This has been evident in physical education and music classes as well as reading, arithmetic, science and language classes.

9. *Self-teaching courses.* Correspondence school courses have been offered in small schools that lack the staff necessary for advanced learning needs of gifted students. Course materials are obtained from correspondence schools or universities by the school officials, with consultation on the part of teachers, students and parents. The selection of such courses will be enhanced if a state, county or regional coordinator for gifted programs serves as a consultant to the small school staff. His help may eliminate the selection of poor correspondence school courses and materials unsuited to the specialized needs of gifted youngsters. The pupils take self-teaching courses unavailable in the regular curriculum. Pupils may work individually or in small groups where they share a common interest or need. They may work under the general direction of a teacher or team of teachers who can guide and direct their activities or provide needed motivation and/or supervision. Pupils who complete correspondence school courses may be given a special examination in order to obtain regular school credit. The correspondence school course is paid for by the school board, not by the pupil.

The correspondence school course may formalize a program based on the encouragement of self-directed activities. In some elementary and secondary schools bright pupils have been encouraged to develop pupil specialties or to work on projects with little if any teacher direction. While this approach has value at all grade levels, the correspondence school course gives the pupils a specific direction and formal work materials for a stated period of time.

10. *The use of community resources.* Many small schools are unable to employ specialists to work with gifted pupils; however, a number of persons who can enrich the lives of gifted students may live or work in the vicinity of the school. For example, one rural community

was able to induce a noted poet to speak regularly with and even work with bright students who showed an interest in poetry. In another community talented musicians were available to give counsel and guidance to talented pupils who showed exceptional interest and ability in one or more phases of music. A third community was able to sponsor a series of speakers from nearby industrial plants; consequently, engineers, scientists, plant managers and technicians provided needed leadership and guidance.

11. *Special programs for bright high school students can be developed with the cooperation of colleges or universities.* Students who live in a city can often find a college that is interested in doing something special for gifted and talented pupils. This is not likely to happen to the boy or girl who lives in a remote rural community, but the door is not closed to these students. With leadership on the part of educators pupils who attend small high schools with limited physical resources and teachers can still engage in activities that will give them new insight and understandings.

The Catskill Area Project illustrates what can be done for rural pupils. For a number of years bright and able or talented high school students from twenty-two schools in three rural counties have been invited to attend weekly seminars on Saturday mornings or in the evenings. The pupils have to travel considerable distances to the cooperating college (State University College of Education) at Oneonta. There the students work with college instructors in one of a number of college-type courses. The students work with specially prepared materials that have been programed for a simple teaching machine. While much of their work calls for research skill or the ability to work independently, the students have an opportunity to work with men, women and fellow students who have ideas and special skills that they can share.

If students cannot take part in a program similar to the Catskill Area Project during the regular school year, they can frequently find colleges that will accept them during the summer when transportation is not likely to be complicated by bad weather. They can thus concentrate all their efforts in a special field of study for six or eight weeks on a college campus. This is not always possible during the regular school term when they have to continue working on regular school assignments. When co-operative programs cannot be developed with a college or university, special Saturday or summer classes for gifted students can be offered in one of the rural high schools. Pupils can go to one of the high schools regularly or they can meet in different schools on a rotation basis. The best qualified instructors can be employed to work with these gifted students in subject fields not generally taught in high school.

12. Pupils may be admitted to higher level courses or classes on the basis of qualifying tests.

8 Conclusion

Recommendations for a More Effective Program for All Children as well as the Gifted

It has been apparent from the foregoing pages that there are a number of approaches to the problem of educating gifted children. Which approach is best is difficult to determine because emotions and personal prejudices get in the way of clear and scientific thinking. In many ways the choice of a program for gifted children depends upon educational philosophy, but in many instances the size of a school and the nature of the community may determine the nature of the program that is ultimately developed. Pressures from outside sources may force educators into programs they do not entirely support or cannot justify with sound evidence.

Essentially, the answer to any program depends upon the quality of the teaching and the richness of the materials available to the teacher and the pupils in the classroom. A special class for gifted children may be the only answer in a school where the regular classroom teacher is bound by rigid grade standards and makes no attempt to provide for individual differences. But, given a staff that understands good grouping principles and the materials necessary for enriching the curriculum, the authors would not hesitate to forego the special class in favor of trying to meet the needs of gifted boys and girls in a heterogeneous setting with subgroup activity and individualization of the program.

The following recommendations for gifted children may appear equally applicable to *all* children. Ideally this is the case. Such a program for all children would guarantee a better program for gifted children.

1. *Boys and girls need to be taught by teachers who have been trained to teach young children.* Boys and girls in the elementary school have a right to work with teachers who have been trained to teach primary, intermediate or upper grade children. Each teacher should know how children learn and what they need in the way of experiences to aid them in the learning process. The teacher should have acquired a rich cultural background plus a command of the techniques necessary for teaching the basic subjects offered in the average elementary school. She should not have to learn how to teach or what to teach as she teaches. She should work with boys and girls because she is interested in their development. This means that, to be successful, she must be able to use sound techniques to discover pupil capacity levels, achievement levels and basic needs. Her teaching must be more than a "high type of hit-or-miss teaching." When she walks about in her community, she should be able to carry her head high because she is a professional person who knows what children need and how to help them realize goals that will help them find their places in a very complex and changing society. To secure such teachers it may be necessary to require a five-year training program for all elementary school teachers with at least one-half year's work in a classroom under the supervision of master teachers, although closed-circuit television and one-way vision screens may have to be the answer to the problem of the teacher shortage.

2. *Schools should be organized to give a continuity of experiences for growing boys and girls extending from kindergarten through high school.* Growth must be con-

tinuous for children as they go from one grade level to another and from one school level to another. Upper grade teachers must be ready and able to build upon the foundations established at lower grade levels. Gifted children, for example, who are introduced to higher-level skills at one level or grade should not have to repeat experiences or wait for others to catch up with them as they move to higher grades. By the same token it is the responsibility of teachers to discover the learning levels of boys and girls who may need further work in essential skill areas of a subject so that they can continue their growth from where they left off with a preceding teacher. Boys and girls should not be pushed into higher learning stages until they are ready for them. Educators must work to eliminate the dual philosophy of education that exists in many school systems. The high school should not feel that its responsibility is to train boys and girls in narrow subject fields primarily in order to get them into college. By the same token the elementary school cannot isolate itself with an all-child-development concept that ignores fundamentals. Both the secondary school and the elementary school are responsible for the development of pupil work standards, interests, attitudes, behavior and academic training. Talent or ability must be recognized in settings that allow for maximum pupil growth at every level of schooling, but maximum development calls for a broad education and not a narrow and selective type of training.

3. *Each elementary school should be organized in terms of flexible teaching units.* Some educators are trying to break with the past by forming ungraded units or through multiclass or multigrade patterns of organization. While these can be steps forward they will not meet the important needs of boys and girls unless something happens in the classroom that is different from what went on in the traditional graded school organization. The grade concept still has its place if children are placed in classrooms where teaching can be flexible.

There are many advantages to the heterogeneous classroom, but heterogeneity can be structured to eliminate extremes at either end of the scale. We should not find slow-learning or gifted children at one end of the intellectual and/or achievement scale who are isolated. By balancing classes we can insure that teachers have teachable groups consisting of pupils who can work together at either end of the scale without being isolated. Here consideration may be given to interest grouping as well as suitability for reading or arithmetic grouping. Teachers will continue to have standards, but they will be flexible standards. Some consideration may be given to the development of multigrade standards—primary, intermediate and upper grade standards in place of grade standards.

4. *Some form of subgrouping is essential for most classes.* Each teacher should be prepared to take children where she finds them in different subject fields. At times this may call for all-class teaching, but because of differences in the way children learn and in the rates of learning teachers must be prepared to use a variety of approaches and materials calling for different levels of instruction. Specific skills will frequently call for some form of interclass grouping or even individualized instruction. Readiness for higher learning activities should dictate how and when children are taught. Many subgroupings will not be permanent since individual differences may be eliminated for some children through teaching based on a recognition of pupil needs. These students may move into new groupings when their problems have been resolved. A unit approach involving the use of many types of committee activity may be considered a form of grouping. Teachers should not be expected to teach extremely retarded children in the regular classroom, but they should be prepared to meet the needs of gifted children by providing them with challenging experiences in the regular classroom.

5. *Entrance into kindergarten or first grade should be flexible enough to allow bright children to enter school*

earlier than average children.* Flexibility in the entering age of children should be permitted in each community depending on the nature of the population in a given school district. Children from high socioeconomic areas may be ready for formal schooling earlier than those from low socioeconomic areas. In the former community a general policy regarding early school admittance may be in order since the entrance age for entering kindergarten and first grade may be lowered three or four months for some pupils without any noticeable effect. This may be done as a blanket policy or by administering individual intelligence tests and adding to it observation or study by trained school personnel. On the other hand, children from underprivileged areas may benefit from a prolonged period of nursery and kindergarten activities; therefore, it is recommended that such children be entered into school earlier where facilities and staff are available with the understanding that they will not be pressured into formal school activities such as are associated with beginning reading and number work. They need a general program that is language- and experience-centered.

Bright or gifted children in average communities should be allowed to start school earlier than average children on the basis of mental maturity, social maturity, emotional maturity and physical maturity. This early acceleration under controlled conditions may take some of the pressures off gifted boys and girls.

6. *Readiness tests and intelligence tests should be administered and evaluated early in the child's school career in order to identify the potentialities of the individual.* Kindergarten or first grade readiness tests are a start in the identification of the gifted and slow-learning children in a school. They may be supplemented by group intelligence tests at the beginning of the first grade as a means of identifying and classifying pupils in terms of their intellectual potential. Other data along with teacher ob-

* Preschool readiness tests may be given as a part of the early identification of the needs of gifted children.

servations will help educators plan a more effective program for those pupils who deviate from the norm. In some instances these pupils may be the ones who receive the benefit of special study to substantiate group test findings.

Lists of children should be prepared; for example, a list of children (a) having mental ages above the 75th percentile or who have IQ's above 120 and (b) having mental ages below the 25th percentile or who have IQ's below 90. Individual intelligence tests should be given to children whose test scores place them at the top or bottom of the intelligence scale. Boys and girls with IQ's below 75 should be considered for special class placement. If such classes are not available care should be taken to refrain from overexposing them to formal instruction until they have had a chance to develop a much higher level of mental maturity.

7. *Teachers should be given help in the identification of exceptional children and their essential needs.* The teacher may be the key to the identification of exceptional children. She should know the characteristics that go with giftedness as well as those that go with mental retardation. If she does not know them, the school administrator and/or supervisor should take steps to help her become familiar with the basic characteristics and needs of such students. An in-service program may inform these teachers through the formation of study groups, through the use of resource people who are specialists in working with exceptional children and through the personal conference approach involving teacher and principal or teacher, principal, specialist and parent. Professional literature may be made available to teachers to aid them in keeping abreast of research findings and practices. Teachers at all levels may need assistance in identifying the needs of these children.

8. *School records should be carefully prepared and maintained for teacher and administrative follow-up or use.* School records that are complete and informative should be prepared. Data on the characteristics, potenti-

alities and needs of individual children should be available for teacher and administrative study. General and meaningless terms should be avoided. Achievement test and intelligence test scores should be supplemented with progress reports from teachers as a pupil goes from grade to grade. Teacher recommendations based on observation and study should become part of a permanent file. Some anecdotal records should become part of the permanent record file when they point out special characteristics, needs, interests, talents or behavior patterns. Results of special programs or studies should be evaluated in terms of other data.

9. *The class size should be controlled so that teachers will have ample opportunity to work closely with their students.* Enrollments of thirty or more are not conducive to an educational program that really meets children's educational needs regardless of their capacity. Decreasing class sizes should be given priority since the best teacher will have trouble getting to know and providing for children's needs when enrollments exceed thirty. A class enrollment ranging from twenty-five to twenty-eight may be considered desirable or even ideal. Recognizing the characteristics and needs of children and planning a program for them is time-consuming and energy-consuming; therefore, class size should be related to the number of pupils to be taught and the number of special teachers available to help teachers in areas such as art, music, physical education, speech and library. One-to-one relationships, sympathetic understanding, individual counseling, adequate planning and attention to specific needs of individuals and groups of children engaged in meaningful experiences become harder and harder to control when class size or special teacher help is ignored.

10. *Teachers must be given the books and teaching tools necessary for children who have many interests and educational needs.* Success with children depends upon having the resources available for them when and where they need them. Each classroom teacher must have the tools for teaching, such as up-to-date textbooks, supple-

mentary readers and other related books to go with basic texts, library books, encyclopedias, dictionaries and other special sources of information including magazines, pamphlets and reports. Materials or equipment essential for conducting experiments or demonstrations should be available to the teacher if they are not actually in the classroom. Children may need to work with games, puzzles and manipulative teaching aids. In addition audiovisual equipment should be available for slides, films, filmstrips, records and tapes. Each school in an educational television center should have television sets available for classroom use. Maps, globes and charts should be basic equipment at every grade level.

11. *Teachers should be prepared to work with children along lines leading to creativity, research, leadership and independent thinking and action.* Teachers must be prepared to work with boys and girls in activities that will promote maximum growth in academic areas and that will lead to creativity, research and independent action and thinking. Children can be trained to assume leadership roles. Teachers must be able to promote research skill through individual and group approaches to the solution of problems. Children will need rich experiences to introduce them to new mediums or new ways to resolve problems. They need to explore the world about them and must have opportunities to experiment with materials or mediums calling for creativity and independent action. Many of the experiences essential for the realization of short- and long-range goals may call for skill in role play, discussion, research, reporting, recording, writing, evaluation and experimentation. The teacher must be familiar with these and other techniques. She must know when to bring all the children together for planning sessions, sharing sessions and evaluation sessions. In addition she has to know how to distinguish between the approaches required for learning by boys and girls who have different experiential backgrounds and capability.

12. *Teachers must be able to allow pupils to go beyond the traditional grade standard concept of learning when*

they are ready and able to find success and understanding with higher-level skills and knowledge. The curriculum should allow for flexibility at each grade level. The program should be one in depth that allows children to make both vertical and horizontal growth. Acceleration as such should be planned in terms of readiness for new and higher-level skills without consideration of actual grade placement. Thus, third grade pupils should not have to continue reading basic third grade readers if they have read widely at this level and have mastered the reading skills normally taught in this grade. They should be allowed to begin work in advanced-level readers when they are ready to use higher-level reading skills, with an understanding that the fourth grade teacher will accept them as students who are ready to work with advanced fourth grade reading materials and skills. Here pupils are allowed to move ahead in a planned acceleration program that allows for vertical growth as they continue to apply the skills and knowledge in a wider exploration of content subjects calling for higher levels of proficiency than is customary in such a grade.

13. *Teachers should make it possible for pupils to acquire new interests as well as extend old interests.* Teachers must be prepared to capitalize upon pupil interests as a means of motivation in the classroom. This means that they must make an effort to identify the natural interests of girls and boys of a certain age level as well as the individual or personal interests of selected students. Again, through opening up new vistas of knowledge teachers can help boys and girls acquire new interests. While many pupils may start a study without any idea of what it is going to be about, a large number of them will end up with new interests as a result of their successes in the new field. Thus, the teacher can use old and new interests to reach higher learning levels.

14. *Teachers should be on the lookout for pupils with special talents.* Teachers have a responsibility to be on the lookout for pupils with talent or who may have a potential for giftedness in selected areas of the curricu-

lum. These boys and girls should be identified so they will not be lost or overlooked as they go through school. Principals may help teachers identify pupils with talents in order to compile a list of outstanding and capable pupils. This listing of pupil talent may become the basis for special classes or special instruction. Where such help is not available in the school, outside agencies may help such students acquire experiences that will allow them to grow in their special fields of interest and skill. In many instances the school can counsel talented pupils and their parents so that growth in the field of giftedness will be continuous. Through flexibility in teacher and pupil schedules talented pupils may be allowed to spend extra time in fields such as art or music with teachers who can give them help when the teacher in their regular classroom cannot do so. In many ways the talented pupils should be allowed to express themselves and to enrich the lives of other pupils without being exploited themselves.

15. *Teachers must be prepared to place increased emphasis upon activities that encourage thinking, planning, experimentation, creativity, problem solving and evaluation.* Gifted children are usually able to memorize fairly easily, so a curriculum based on mere memorization of rules, facts and unrelated bits of information is not truly challenging to them. These individuals must go beyond rote learning if they are going to mature to their fullest limits. They are capable of working with many types of abstractions, but they need rich experiences that will help them develop their powers of observation and thinking. They have to engage in activities that encourage problem-solving, thinking in terms of abstractions, planning, organizing, experimenting, creating and evaluation. They need to be able to gather information before making generalizations; then they must be prepared to test them. For success at high levels they must be able to (a) read widely in content areas, (b) discuss and solve problems on the basis of reasoning or thought, (c) engage in creative thinking and activities and (d) engage in activities that enable them to assume leadership roles.

16. *Teachers should maintain close contacts with parents.* Education is a joint responsibility of parents and teachers. Each one has something to contribute to the other about the growing boy or girl. Parent conferences should be encouraged at all grade levels for a deeper understanding of the problems and progress of individual children. There should be a feeling of mutual respect between the home and the school if children are to grow in a stimulating and challenging environment. Parents should understand the goals and purposes of the school if they are to support it.

17. *Teachers should make as much use of community resources as possible.* Teachers should be ready to take their children into the community to take advantage of resources that are not available in the classroom. Field trips often give the boys and girls new firsthand experiences but, more important, in many instances they become the basis for increased learning and understanding that is impossible where books alone are the vehicle for promoting growth and understanding. Children at every grade level should become familiar with an ever-expanding community until by the time they reach high school they are familiar with the resources and institutions at state and national levels. Resource people should be used by the classroom teacher where they can give enrichment and depth to a program. If teachers will look around, they will find many individuals and many agencies ready and willing to help if called upon.

18. *Gifted children should have someone they can go to for counsel or help.* Since there is often a crying need in many high school guidance staffs and facilities, it is difficult to find sympathy and support for guidance at lower grade levels. While the homeroom guidance plan has many supporters at the junior high level, every large elementary school as well as every junior high school should have one or more trained staff members who can talk to boys and girls about their problems. Young children can often talk out their problems with a regular teacher, but she is not always trained or qualified to give

help to those who have problems, real or imaginary. Frequently they do not know to whom they can turn for help. In many instances boys and girls may not need much more than assurance that someone is there to help them; at other times their personal problems may overwhelm them. In small elementary schools the school nurse and the principal may have opportunities to listen to pupil problems, which helps teachers understand the basic needs of their charges; but in large elementary schools children miss the personal contacts so essential for understanding.

19. *An enrichment coordinator should be available to supervise, help plan and direct activities in a school or school system.* Many small schools cannot secure funds for adequate classroom teachers, so the idea of an enrichment coordinator may be a form of daydreaming. In such schools the principal or supervisor often has to help encourage teachers to sponsor enrichment activities but state and county educational leadership can still be directed along these lines to supplement what is done by the principal. In larger schools or school systems an enrichment coordinator may be employed to help teachers identify children in terms of their potentialities and their basic needs. Activities can be planned, materials secured and techniques taught, all of which will give new meaning and life to the ongoing activities found in the regular classroom. Through group and individual meetings with the teachers the enrichment coordinator can help teachers grow as they help children grow. They would be resource people rather than special teachers. They would assist teachers but not supplant them.

20. *Teachers should be encouraged to experiment with new techniques and new teaching materials in the light of pupil needs and capacities.* So much has been said about accelerating learning that we forget that many gifted children do not need acceleration as much as they need time and opportunity to get thoroughly acquainted with the world about them. We hear about new mathematics programs or new science programs. These are entirely new

fields of study based upon new advances or understandings. In many instances they require new concepts of teaching and new understanding on the part of the instructor. In a sense education is in a process of revolution but before there can be wide acceptance of these new ideas teachers must be free to experiment with both the ideas and the techniques. In some instances teachers will have to learn to adjust to new educational concepts or educational philosophies if they are going to test thoroughly the advantages of such innovations as team teaching, program learning, television teaching, the use of the language laboratory, speed reading, individualized reading and other innovations yet to come as educators learn to apply science to the improvement of the teaching and learning situation for children of different abilities.

Bibliography

Abraham, Willard, *Common Sense About Gifted Children.* New York: Harper and Brothers, 1958.

Anderson, K. E. (ed.), *Research on the Academically Talented Student.* Washington, D.C.: National Education Association, 1961.

Armstrong, William H., *Study Is Hard Work.* New York: Harper and Brothers, 1957.

Barbe, Walter B., "Are Gifted Children Being Adequately Provided For?" *Educational Administration and Supervision,* 40 (November, 1954).

———, "Evaluation of Special Classes for Gifted Children." *Exceptional Children,* 22 (November, 1955).

Braun, R. H., "Three Experiments in Staff Utilization at Urbana, Homogeneous Grouping, and Acceleration," National Association of Secondary School Principals *Bulletin,* 43 (January, 1959).

Brown, Spencer, "How to Educate the Gifted Child." *Commentary,* 21 (1956).

Bruner, J. S., *The Process of Education.* Cambridge, Mass.: Harvard University Press, 1960.

Bryan, J. Ned, *Talent—A State's Resource, A State's Responsibility.* Washington, D.C.: U.S. Government Printing Office, 1963.

Charles, Don C., *Psychology of the Child in the Classroom.* New York: The Macmillan Company, 1964.

Cutts, N. E., and N. Mosley, *Teaching the Bright and Gifted.* Englewood Cliffs, N.J.: Prentice-Hall, Inc., 1957.

DeHaan, R. F., and Robert J. Havighurst, *Educating Gifted*

Children. Chicago, Ill.: University of Chicago Press, 1957.

Dinkmeyer, D., and R. Dreikurs, *Encouraging Children to Learn.* Englewood Cliffs, N.J.: Prentice-Hall, Inc., 1963.

Drews, Elizabeth M., "A Critical Evaluation of Approaches to the Identification of Gifted Students." In A. Traxler (ed.), *Measurement and Evaluation in Today's Schools.* Washington, D.C.: American Council on Education, 1961.

————, "Recent Findings About Gifted Adolescents." In E. Paul Torrance (ed.), *New Educational Ideas: Third Minnesota Conference on Gifted Children.* Minneapolis: Center for Continuation Study, University of Minnesota, 1961.

Ducanis, Alex J., "Advanced Placement in New York State, a Follow-up Study," The University of the State of New York, The State Education Department, Division of Research in Higher Education, 1965.

Dunn, Lloyd M. (ed.), *Exceptional Children in the Schools.* New York: Holt, Rinehart and Winston, Inc. 1963.

Durr, William K., "The Gifted Child," *Michigan Education Journal,* 37 (October, 1959).

————, "Provisions for the Gifted in Relation to School Size and System Size at the Elementary Level," *The Journal of Educational Research,* 55 (December–January, 1962).

————, *The Gifted Student.* New York: Oxford University Press, 1964.

Engle, Thelburn L., "Achievements of Pupils Who Have Had Double Promotions in Elementary School," *Elementary School Journal,* 36 (November, 1935).

————, "A Study of the Effects of School Acceleration Upon the Personality and School Adjustment of High School and University Students," *Journal of Educational Psychology,* 29 (October, 1938).

Frankel, E., "The Gifted Academic Underachiever," *Science Teacher,* 28 (1961).

Freehill, Maurice F., *Gifted Children.* New York: The Macmillan Company, 1961.

Freitas, Anthony V., "Gifted Fifth Graders in a Class by Themselves," The Instructor, 69 (May, 1960).

French, Joseph L., "The Preparation of Teachers of the

Gifted," *The Journal of Teacher Education,* 12 (March, 1961).

———, "Reactions of Gifted Elementary Pupils," *The Gifted Child,* 2 (Fall, 1958).

Fund for the Advancement of Education, *Bridging the Gap Between School and College,* Chapter V. New York: The Fund, 1953.

———, "Report on Fourth Year of Experiment in Early Admission at Goucher College," 1954–55. Towson, Maryland: Goucher College, 1956. Mimeographed.

Gallagher, J. J., *Analysis of Research on the Education of Gifted Children.* Springfield, Ill.: Office of the Superintendent of Public Instruction, 1960.

———, *Teaching the Gifted Child.* Boston, Mass.: Allyn & Bacon, 1964. Getzels, Jacob W., and Philip W. Jackson, *Creativity and Intelligence.* New York: John Wiley and Sons, Inc., 1962.

———, "The Study of Giftedness: A Multidimensional Approach," *The Gifted Student.* Cooperative Research Monograph No. 2, U.S. Department of Health, Education and Welfare, Office of Education. Washington, D.C.: U.S. Government Printing Office, 1960.

Goldberg, Miriam L., "Research on the Talented." Bureau of Publications, Teachers College, Columbia University. New York, 1965.

Gowan, J. C., "Recent Research on the Education of Gifted Children," *Psychological Newsletter,* 9 (March, 1958).

Gray, Edward A., "Some Factors in the Undergraduate Career of Young College Students," *Contributions to Education,* No. 437. New York: Bureau of Publications, Teachers College, Columbia University, 1930.

Guilford, J. P., "Structure of Intellect," *Psychological Bulletin,* 53 (1956).

———, "Three Faces of Intellect," *The American Psychologist,* 14, No. 8 (August, 1959).

———, *Personality.* New York: McGraw-Hill Book Company, 1959.

———, "Factorial Angles to Psychology," *Psychological Review,* 68 (1961).

Gunn, H. M., "The Gifted Child and the Responsibility of the Elementary Principal," *Journal of Educational Research,* 26 (May, 1958).

Havighurst, R. J., *et al.*, *A Survey of the Education of Gifted Children*. Chicago, Ill.: The University of Chicago Press, 1955.

Hildreth, Gertrude, "Characteristics of Young Gifted Children," *Journal of Genetic Psychology*, 53 (1938).

Hobson, James R., "Mental Age as a Workable Criterion for School Admission," *Elementary School Journal*, 48 (February, 1948).

Holland, John L., "Creative and Academic Performance Among Talented Adolescents," *Journal of Educational Psychology*, 52 (August, 1961).

Hollingworth, Harry, *Mental Growth and Decline*. New York: D. Appleton and Company, 1927.

Howard, Jane, "The Nicest Young Genius in the U.S.," *Life*, 58 (May 21, 1965).

Hutchinson, Michael, and C. Young, *Educating the Intelligent*. Baltimore, Md.: Penguin Books, 1962.

Jencks, Christopher, "Segregating the Gifted," *The New Republic*, 150 (April 25, 1964).

Justman, Joseph, "Academic Achievement of Intellectually Gifted Accelerants and Non-Accelerants in Junior High School," *School Review*, 62 (March, 1954).

———, "Personal and Social Adjustments of Intellectually Gifted Accelerants and Non-Accelerants in Junior High School," *School Review*, 61 (November, 1953).

Justman, Joseph, and J. Wayne Wrightstone, "The Expressed Attitudes of Teachers Toward Special Classes for Intellectually Gifted Children," *Educational Administration and Supervision*, 42 (March, 1956).

Keys, Noel, "Adjustments of Under Age Students in High School," *Psychological Bulletin*, 32 (October, 1935).

Lange-Eichbaum, Wilhelm, *The Problem of Genius*. New York: The Macmillan Company, 1932.

Laycock, Samuel, *Gifted Children: A Handbook for the Classroom Teacher*. Toronto, Canada: The Copp Clark Publishing Company, 1957.

Lease, J., and L. A. Fliegler, "Problems and Practices," in Louis A. Fliegler (ed.), *Curriculum Planning for the Gifted*. Englewood Cliffs, N.J.: Prentice-Hall, Inc., 1961.

Lewis, Gertrude M., *Educating the More Able Children in Grades Four, Five and Six*. Washington, D.C.: U.S. Government Printing Office, 1961.

Lorge, Irving, "Social Gains in the Special Education of the Gifted," *School and Society*, 79 (January, 1954).

Magary, James, and John R. Eichorn (eds.), *The Exceptional Child*. New York: Holt, Rinehart and Winston, Inc., 1960.

McConnell, T. R., "Educational Articulation," *Journal of Higher Education*, 5 (1934).

Mead, Margaret, "Be Glad Your Child Is Different," *Parent's Magazine*, 39 (September, 1964).

Mirman, Norman, "Are Accelerated Students Socially Maladjusted?" *Elementary School Journal*, 62 (1962).

Morris, Glyn, "Helping the Mentally Superior Child in Rural Areas," *Exceptional Children*, 22 (January, 1956).

Nason, Leslie J., *Academic Achievement of Gifted High School Students*. Los Angeles: University of Southern California Press, 1958.

National Association of Secondary School Principals, *Administration: Procedures and School Practices for the Academically Talented Student in the Secondary School*. Washington, D.C.: National Education Association, 1960.

National Education Association, *Elementary Education and the Academically Talented Pupil*. Washington, D.C., 1961.

National Education Association Project on the Academically Talented Student and American Personnel and Guidance Association, *Guidance for the Academically Talented Student*, Elizabeth M. Drews (ed.). Washington, D.C.: National Education Association, 1961.

Norris, Dorothy E., "Programs in the Elementary Schools," *Education for the Gifted*, The Fifty-Seventh Yearbook of the National Society for the Study of Education, Part II (N. B. Henry, ed.). Chicago, Ill.: The University of Chicago Press, 1958.

Otto, Henry J. (ed.), *Curriculum Enrichment for Gifted Elementary School Children in Regular Classes*. Austin, Texas: Bureau of Laboratory Schools, University of Texas, 1957.

Paschal, Elizabeth, *Encouraging the Excellent*. New York: The Fund for the Advancement of Education, 1962.

Passow, A. Harry, "Enrichment of Education for the Gifted," *Education for the Gifted*. The Fifty-Seventh Yearbook of the National Society for the Study of Education, Part II

(N. B. Henry, ed.). Chicago, Ill.: University of Chicago Press, 1958.

Piaget, J., *The Psychology of Intelligence*. London, Eng.: Routledge and Kegan Paul, 1951.

———, *Language and Thought of the Child*. New York: Meridian, 1955.

"Put Away Your Blocks," *Time*, 84 (October 9, 1964).

Reynolds, M. C., "Acceleration," in E. Paul Torrance (ed.), *Talent and Education*. Minneapolis: University of Minnesota Press, 1960.

Riessman, F., *The Culturally Deprived Child*. New York: Harper & Row, 1962.

Roberts, Fran, "The Gifted Child," *American Mercury*, 92 (January, 1961).

Rosenbloom, P. C. (ed.), *Modern Viewpoints in the Curriculum*. New York: McGraw-Hill Book Company, 1964.

Seashore, Carl, *The Discovery and Guidance of Musical Talent*. National Society for the Study of Education, Vol. 34. Chicago, Ill.: University of Chicago Press, 1935.

Shane, Harold G., "Grouping in the Elementary School," *Phi Delta Kappa*, 41 (April, 1960).

Sumption, Merle R., and Evelyn M. Luecking, *Education of the Gifted*. New York: The Ronald Press, 1960.

Taylor, C. W., "Who Are the Exceptionally Creative?" *Exceptional Children*, 28 (1962).

——— (ed.), *Creativity: Progress and Potential*. New York: McGraw-Hill Book Company, 1964.

Terman, Lewis M., *et al.*, *Genetic Studies of Genius*. Vol. I: *Mental and Physical Traits of a Thousand Gifted Children*, 1925. Vol. II: *The Early Mental Traits of Three Hundred Geniuses*, 1926. Vol. III: *The Promise of Youth, Follow-up Studies of a Thousand Gifted Children*, 1930. Vol. IV: *The Gifted Child Grows Up, Twenty-Five Years' Follow-up of a Superior Group*, 1947. Vol. V: *The Gifted Group at Mid-Life, Thirty-five Years' Follow-up of the Superior Child*, 1959. Stanford, Calif.: Stanford University Press.

Terman, Lewis M., and Melita H. Oden, *The Gifted Child Grows Up, Twenty-Five Years' Follow-up of a Superior Group*, Vol. IV. In *Genetic Studies of Genius*. Stanford, Calif.: Stanford University Press, 1947.

Torrance, E. Paul (ed.), *Talent and Education*. Minneapolis: University of Minnesota Press, 1960.

———, *Education and the Creative Potential*. Minneapolis: The University of Minnesota Press, 1963.

———, *Gifted Children in the Classroom*. New York: The Macmillan Company, 1965.

"Triple Speed Learning," *Time*, 81 (January 11, 1963).

Wampler, N. Norman, "Bellflower Challenges the Gifted," *The American School Board Journal*, 131 (August, 1955).

Ward, Virgil S., *Educating the Gifted: An Axiomatic Approach*. Columbus, Ohio: Charles E. Merrill Books, 1961.

Warren, Matthew M., "Speeding Up the Bright Ones," *Atlantic Monthly*, 209 (June, 1962).

West, Jeff, "Teaching the Talented," Bulletin #1-A, Dade County Public Schools, Miami, Florida, *c.* 1960.

Wilkins, Laray, "High School Achievement of Accelerated Pupils," *School Review*, 44 (April, 1936).

Williams, Meta F., "Acceptance and Performance Among Gifted Elementary School Children," *Educational Research Bulletin*, 37 (November, 1958).

Witty, Paul, "How to Identify the Gifted," *Childhood Education*, Vol. 29, No. 7 (March, 1953).

———, "Who Are the Gifted?" *Education for the Gifted*, Chapter III. The Fifty-Seventh Yearbook of the National Society for the Study of Education, Part II. Chicago, Ill.: The University of Chicago Press, 1958.

Witty, Paul A. (ed.), *The Gifted Child*. Boston, Mass.: D. C. Heath & Company, 1951.

———, "The Gifted and the Creative Student," *School and Society*, 92 (April 18, 1964).

Woolcock, Cyril W., *New Approaches to the Education of the Gifted*. Morristown, New Jersey: Silver Burdett Company, 1961.

Worcester, Dean A., *The Education of Children of Above Average Mentality*. Lincoln: University of Nebraska Press, 1955.

Index

GEORGE I. THOMAS has been an elementary and secondary school teacher, principal, superintendent of schools and professor of education. He is presently research consultant with the State Education Department in Albany, New York, and is in charge of several experimental programs in education in New York State. Dr. Thomas obtained his M.A. (1940) and the Ed.D. (1951) from Teachers College, Columbia University. He has published in *American School Board Journal, Elementary School Journal, Nation's Schools,* and *National Elementary Principal.*

JOSEPH CRESCIMBENI has been an elementary and secondary school teacher, college and university professor, and curriculum consultant. He is now an Associate Professor of Graduate Elementary Education at Jacksonville University, Florida. He received his M.A. from Fitchburg State (Mass.) in 1950 and his Ph.D. from the University of Connecticut in 1964. Dr. Crescimbeni has published widely in educational journals including the *NEA Journal, Saturday Review, Education, Child and Family, The Arithmetic Teacher* and *Phi Delta Kappa.* He has also co-authored a book on American education and has written two books on teaching the new mathematics.